Twayne's United States Authors Series

EDITOR OF THIS VOLUME

Lewis Leary

University of North Carolina

John Neal

TUSAS 307

John Neal

JOHN NEAL

By DONALD A. SEARS

California State University, Fullerton

TWAYNE PUBLISHERS

A DIVISION OF G. K. HALL & CO., BOSTON

Copyright © 1978 by G. K. Hall & Co.

Published in 1978 by Twayne Publishers,
A Division of G. K. Hall & Co.
All Rights Reserved

Printed on permanent/durable acid-free paper and bound
in the United States of America

First Printing

Library of Congress Cataloging in Publication Data

Sears, Donald A
John Neal.

(Twayne's United States authors series ; TUSAS 307)
Bibliography: p. 145-50
Includes index.
1. Neal, John, 1793-1876. 2. Authors, American
—19th century—Biography.
PS2459.N28Z85   813'.2 [B]   78-5224
ISBN 0-8057-7230-8

For Oretta

who as wife and lawyer fulfills Neal's dream—and mine—of
a new American woman

Contents

About the Author

Donald A. Sears was, like John Neal, born Down-East in Portland, Maine, going as far away as Bowdoin College to receive his B.A. (*magna cum laude*). He received his M.A. and Ph.D. from Harvard University. At present Dr. Sears is Professor of English and Linguistics at California State University, Fullerton, where he teaches a variety of courses including a seminar in American romanticism.

Dr. Sears is former Executive Director of the College English Association and editor of its publications. He was Director of the Book-of-the-Month-Club Creative Writing Fellowship program, and has himself published his poetry and translations in the journals. He is the author of numerous articles on American literature and linguistics. His books include *The Harbrace Guide to the Library and Research Paper* and *The Discipline of English*.

Preface

John Neal has long held a tiny but secure place in histories of American literature as an early novelist and critic, but his reputation has suffered from the unavailability of his works and from a scarcity of studies of them. The four-volume dissertation of Irving T. Richards has remained in a single copy in the archives of Harvard University, and until 1972 there was no full-scale published biography. Excellent as is Benjamin Lease's study, it is his purpose to focus on Neal's role as literary nationalist, and therefore relatively slight treatment is given to Neal's activities as reformer, art and theater critic, and patron of budding talent. The present study has the advantage of previous scholarship and may accordingly attempt a fuller and more balanced assessment of Neal's long and immensely varied career.

In particular this book places Neal in the intellectual milieu of northern New England in the early nineteenth century; for his style—both personal and literary—is pure Yankee in both virtues and faults. He is a forerunner in utilizing dialect (what he called "talking on paper") for literary purposes, and this contribution to American colloquial style is developed in detail. He was also among the first to demonstrate that native materials of the colonies and the Revolution may be made viable for fiction.

Among the perpetuated misjudgments of John Neal has been the myth of a quarrelsome man who finally destroyed his talent by burying himself in his home town of Portland, Maine. But the myth has failed both to detect the sensitive, talented, self-made American beneath the self-advertised mask of a Byronic Yankee and to estimate correctly the cultural level of Portland in the years before the Civil War. Reassessment reveals the pioneer who prepared the fields of criticism and fiction for such followers as Hawthorne and Poe, and who in his flamboyant way demonstrated that the life of a literary man in our new nation may be an honorable calling. Beneath his posings, Neal was a perceptive discoverer of talent and a brilliant if erratic editor as well as poet, dramatist, novelist, critic, and reformer-lecturer. Hopefully, the whole man will emerge from the following pages, and we will see something like the total impact of that northern meteor of letters—John Neal.

If the author has succeeded, it is in large part because of the labors of those who have gone before him. For every scholar climbs by a path hewn by his predecessors. But there always remains much labor of digging, clearing of underbrush, and throwing of bridges of conjecture across the voids until he reaches his partial goal, a plateau of vantage from whence to view his subject in unobstructed light. To all his predecessors—known and acknowledged or unknown—go the thanks of one who comprehends their enormous work. One who seeks the path to the truth about John Neal assumes special debts of gratitude to the trailblazing of Fred Lewis Pattee, to the spade work of the late Irving T. Richards, and to the bridge-building of such current scholars as Benjamin Lease and Hans-Joachim Lang. His wandering steps have also been steadied by those resourceful guides, the research librarians of Harvard University, the Library of Congress, the New York Public Library, the Portland Public Library, the Maryland Historical Society, the Maine Historical Society, and the library of his home university.

The author also wishes to acknowledge the patient understanding of Sylvia Bowman, editor of the series, who has waited without complaint ten years for him to fulfill his desire to do justice to John Neal. If less than justice is done in the following pages, the failure is not hers. Nor is it that of the author's wife, Oretta Ferri Sears, who has patiently learned more about John Neal than she ever wanted to know. For final and accurate preparation of the manuscript, his thanks are due Mrs. Sherrill Pieschel. And for providing a resonant sounding board of criticism and help, the students of his seminar in American romanticism are reserved a special share of the path of knowledge we all climb.

Finally, completion of the writing was greatly facilitated by a sabbatical leave and a grant from California State University, Fullerton.

DONALD SEARS

California State University, Fullerton

Chronology

1832	Writes for *Atlantic Souvenir*. Gains inheritance from bachelor uncle, James Neal.
1833	*The Down-Easters*, a novel. Travels to New York and to the West.
1834	June 11, daughter Margaret Eleanor born.
1835	Editor of the *New England Galaxy* in which appears *Our Ephraim* (a play). Publishes in *The Token, New England Magazine, Portland Magazine*.
1836	Publishes in *The Token, Portland Magazine*. Receives masters degree from Bowdoin College.
1837	*Banks and Banking*
1840	January—April, editor of *The New World*.
1843	May—December, editor of *Brother Jonathan. Ruth Elder, a* serial novel.
1844	October 17, daughter Eleanor born.
1845	New York Tabernacle address on Women's Rights. September 17, daughter Eleanor dies.
1847	November 29, son John Pierpont born.
1848	June—July, editor of *Portland Transcript*.
1849	December 11, mother dies.
1851	Joins Congregational Church, High Street, with wife and sister.
1854	*One Word More*, a religious statement.
1856	August 26, son James dies.
1858	May 18, sister Rachel dies.
1859	*True Womanhood*, a novel.
1863	*The White-Faced Pacer*.
1864	*The Moose-Hunter*.
1866	*Little Moccasin*. Death of John Pierpont; great fire in Portland.
1869	*Wandering Recollections*, an autobiography.
1870	*Great Mysteries and Little Plagues*, a juvenile.
1874	*Portland Illustrated*, a history.
1876	John Neal dies, June 20.

CHAPTER 1

Yankee Genius as a Young Man

A young journalist in 1833 wrote that "Neal is an American, heart and soul. He is a Yankee, proud of his country and his country-men. . . . His books are of an American hue. . . . I ask if a writer of so much originality and strength, who has contributed abroad and at home, so much to the formation of an American literature, shall be passed over in silence among those whom we are proud of?"[1] Already in the 1830s the reputation of John Neal was in eclipse and in need of defense, for he lived to be surpassed by men of lesser genius but greater control of their talents. His voice from the Maine frontier was that of a forerunner and trailblazer, and thus a proper evaluation of John Neal's literary achievements depends on seeing him in the perspective of his generation, the first to be born in the newly independent United States. Only two of the group closest to him in age were to overshadow him—Cooper in fiction and Bryant in poetry. Otherwise he compares well with the humor and folklore of a Seba Smith, the oratory and frontier material of an Augustus Longstreet and James Hall, or the romancing of a John Pendleton Kennedy. Ten years his senior, Washington Irving stood out before him, as Emerson, ten years his junior, towered after him. But the giants of the American Renaissance—Simms, Longfellow, Whittier, Poe, Holmes, Lowell, Thoreau, Melville, Whitman—were all born after Neal's boyhood closed and after he had commenced working for a living.

Neal had few American examples to help him in his production of a native literature, for he was of the pioneer generation who attempted to acclimatize contemporary British romanticism to the American milieu. Byron was only five years his senior, twenty-nine to Neal's twenty-four, when the budding American author reviewed *Childe Harold* in the pages of *The Portico*. Shelley and Keats were close contemporaries.

A new ferment of revolutionary and romantic doctrines was having
its effect on the generation born at the turn of the eighteenth century.
In the settled towns of the East Coast, peace and prosperity gave
impetus to literary and artistic yearnings. Even the northern regional
center of Falmouth—later Portland[2]—reacted to the new stirrings.
The soil had been prepared by two hundred years of settlement and
needed only the leisure and wealth, the drive of literary nationalism,
and the excitement of romanticism to yield an indigenous crop of
literary masterpieces. John Neal was born too soon to be part of the
true American Renaissance, but was a ground breaker of the newly
fertile literary land. Like his younger New England contemporaries,
his own roots went back to the beginnings of the colonies. He was a
sixth generation son of the territory north of Boston, for the first John
Neal (Neial) had landed in Boston about 1650, as a bond servant and
prisoner of war. He had been one of the royalist Scots defeated by
Cromwell at the Battle of Dunbar in 1650 and subsequently settled in
the New World. Following service in the saw mills and iron works of
Lynn, Massachusetts, he was granted land near Berwick, Maine,
where he raised his family and died in 1704. Continuing to farm in the
Berwick and Eliot area of southern Maine, the Neals were by the
early eighteenth century associated with the Society of Friends
(Quakers), John's grandfather James Neal being a Quaker preacher.
This heritage was doubled when James' son John married Rachel
Hall, a descendant of the prolific Quaker (Neal speaks of a thousand
descendants) Hatevil Hall. At the time of John's birth in 1793, the
Halls and Neals were settled in Portland.[3]

John Neal was thus born into the close-knit Quaker society of
Portland. As early as 1730 the first of the sect had settled in the area,
and by 1782 leaders of the conservative Congregational church were
fulminating against their increase especially when "great numbers
flocked" to the Quakers' annual meeting.[4] While there was no
outright persecution of the sect, it was a visible minority in the town;
a sensitive and poor boy, held to the Quaker dress code, stood out at
the public school. Even seventy years later Neal recalled the taunts
and bullying of fellow students, an experience that reinforced his
sense of uniqueness as well as his quick belligerence. Later drummed
out of the Society in Baltimore, Neal retained an ambivalent feeling
for his birthright sect. They had been supportive of his mother in her
struggling widowhood, but their slowness in adapting to change
made them appear narrow and often ridiculous. In his fiction,

Quakers are frequently the subject of comedy or satire,[5] but equally a Rachel Dyer is set forth as a true heroine. Neal's heritage is thus like that of his admired Charles Brockden Brown, a Quaker by birth whose interest in the mystic came from this source, and like that of his distant kinsman John Greenleaf Whittier, with whom he shared an interest in local scenes.

I Down-East Roots

John Neal was born on August 25, 1793, twelve hours after his twin sister Rachel; they were the only children of John and Rachel Neal, for whom they were named, for the father died when the twins were a month old. Young John's education was conducted by his mother, who took over her husband's teaching profession, and by an occasional helping hand of discipline from Uncle James Neal, his father's unmarried brother.

Public school days followed as an introduction to the school of hard knocks, until John learned to deny his Quaker training and to fight back against the bullies. A brief interlude at a Quaker school in Windham, Maine, was remembered for the misery of his existence there. At twelve his formal schooling was over; he took his first job as a retail clerk in the store of Munroe and Tuttle of Portland. There he learned the sharp practice of passing off counterfeit bills to backwoods innocents. When the firm failed in 1807—one of many casualties of the Embargo Act—John took employment with the store of Benjamin Willis at a salary of forty dollars a year plus board and washing. When it in turn failed, he joined an itinerant teacher of penmanship in a tour Down East, adding portraiture to his other skills of the hand.

In answer to an advertisement, he entered the drygoods store of a Mr. Murphy of Boston, where his salary was a handsome eighty dollars a year. For a brief spell he set up on his own in the wholesale trade before meeting and joining in partnership with Joseph Lord and his brother-in-law John Pierpont. The partnership gave Neal his first and most lasting friendship with the slightly older Pierpont. Together they had grandiose ideas for a mercantile chain of stores, expanding southward to Baltimore and thence to Charleston. But by 1816, they were bankrupt. The crash led Pierpont to the ministry and Neal, to law and literature. With the success of published novels, poetry, and a play behind him, Neal sailed for England in late 1823. There he broke into the journals—notably *Blackwood's*—with articles on American authors and artists. His novel *Brother Jonathan* was, however, unsuccessful. After a period spent in the home of Jeremy Bentham, he returned to the United States, with the intention of settling in New York City.

He was in the midst of life and career, with the rugged good looks of his Scot ancestry. Light-colored silky hair formed in natural ringlets around a fine head and high forehead. Sparkling blue eyes commanded attention. His five feet eight or nine inches was sufficient height to carry his robust and athletic frame. He was, wrote one observer, "a man to make a statue of, every limb was so well developed, and there was so much of manhood in the whole figure."[6] He was, however, no statue, but a bundle of bounding energy, always in motion. On a visit home, he was met with scorn and abuse for his English articles and his hometown portrait in *Randolph*. New York was forgotten, and he determined, out of sheer perversity, to settle in Portland. He would force his way into the Maine bar, and succeed just because they said he could not. There, in his hometown, Neal lived from 1827 to his death in 1869, editing, publishing, and prospering.[7]

Far from being the dead land where he wasted or buried his talents, the Portland of John Neal was indeed a provincial capital of exciting growth and substantial cultural aspirations.[8] After two abortive starts in the colonial period—the seventeenth-century settlement was abandoned in 1690 because of Indian warfare, and the second settlement was burned early in the Revolution by the bombardment of Captain Mowat[9]—a new and vital beginning coincided with Independence. Neal's own fervor for literary nationalism was a reflection of the local fervor on the Maine frontier. At the time of his birth Portland was the most important town in the territory; with well over two thousand inhabitants the town boasted its own newspaper and library. In 1794 the theater presented Shakespeare.

By 1810—in spite of financial reverses caused by the Embargo Act—the population showed a ninety-three percent increase to over seven thousand, bringing the town into fifteenth place in the nation according to size. By the time of Neal's return from England, Portland was the capital of the new state of Maine, bustling with ships that plied the seven seas and wagons that emptied the produce of the back country of New Hampshire. By 1830 the wagons were supplemented by the boats of the Oxford Canal that opened a waterway from the White Mountains to the port. The population was nearing thirteen thousand as incorporation as a city took place in

1832. During the entire period from 1810 to 1840 Portland ranked as one of the twenty-five largest cities in the country. It was in this regional center that John Neal lived most of his days, in the expansive atmosphere between the two destructions of the city of Portland—the first in 1775 by British bombardment and the second by a disastrous fire in 1866.

The city itself was a place of natural beauty, its saddle-shaped peninsula overlooking the hundreds of pine-clad islands of Casco Bay to the east and the White Mountains to the west. A naturally deep harbor opened on the shortest sea route to Europe. Portland flourished with the shipping trade of its merchant class. But tensions and ferment strove beneath the calm and beauty. Eighteenth-century ways lingered on among the upper class, but frontier de-mocracy also jostled to be recognized. The young John Neal sympathized with these Whiggish frontier elements even as he vowed to win a place among the Longfellows and Mellens of the Federalist ruling caste. At thirteen he could sympathize with the local editor Nathaniel Willis, Jr., who was thrown in jail on libel charges—one of the first to fight for freedom of the press under the new Bill of Rights. [10] His son N. P. Willis and daughter "Fanny Fern" were to grow to be authors of the more genteel sort—accepted where their father was not.

Willis's true heir was the turbulent and outspoken John Neal, whose own restless activity was a product of tensions—tensions between his own athletic prowess and the feminine influence of a teaching mother and an unmarried sister: of America versus England; of Portland of the north and Baltimore of the south; of the poor boy who became a rich man; of the self-educated man who lived to be the mentor of Poe, Whittier, Hawthorne, and Longfellow. Out of these tensions came his fixed principle to always do what others felt him incapable of doing: ". . . with languages, literature, law, and poetry, the mere spirit of contradiction—the desire to do what my best friends believed me incapable of—has done more for me than any and all other influences. . . ."[11] This "spirit of contradiction"—a wilful acting contrariwise to expectation—was both the spark to his genius and a nearly self-destructive force. He burst upon the literary scene, seemingly self-assured, loud, and ready to quarrel.

Thus, from his own time to ours, Neal's reputation has always suffered by the confusion he himself produced in readers. It is hard to take him with sufficient seriousness, for he is brash, noisy, cantankerous, cocksure, at least in the public image that he created for himself. And there is the problem of tone: he mocks his own style and undercuts himself in his introductions and self-reviews. At times he cannot resist a pun or a self-parody. He seems determined to flaunt his faults and demand that they be considered virtues. For example, when the reception of the first edition of the *Battle of Niagara* was going well, he added a note to the introduction to the second edition in which he confesses that he had not been aware that the first part of the title poem had not been written in iambic pentameter. In the same introduction he relates at large his failure on the lecture platform in Philadelphia, using his own disappointment as a springboard for an attack on the cultural obtuseness of the city. And he depreciates the shorter poems with which he enlarged the second edition, stating that he only included them so as to have a handy and portable copy near him.

But it is not candor or self-depreciation that comes through from these comments. What could have been disarming modesty carries instead the tone of brawling egotism; and this is unfortunate, for there is a private Neal who has eluded the critics. The poor boy who had been deprived of formal education after the age of twelve was painfully sensitive. He developed a defense mechanism that taught him to attack, to avoid the probable slight by striking first. The public image obscures the private man: Neal the family man, closest to his mother and unmarried twin sister, both school teachers; Neal the lover of few friends, but constant to the one close friend, Pierpont, for all his adult years; Neal the father, hurt to the depths of his being by the tragedy of his eldest son's alcoholism and early death; Neal, the unstinting champion of young talent—all these hide behind the Byronic superman image that he created for himself through his fictional heroes. Nor is his autobiography any help, for it is disorganized and deals with the public man, still vending advertisements for himself. The private papers and personal letters were turned to ashes in the great fire of Portland in 1866, thus forcing the critic to read between the lines, to try to listen to the intervals of quiet amid the rant, and to come finally to grips with a highly sensitive human being who cares desperately for the underdog, as he himself had been an underdog—the serious literary man with a developed literary theory to support his writing and his criticism. There is little help from Neal himself in such a search, and few have taken the time and trouble. One key lies in his lifelong habit of reading, the poor boy's source of self-education.

II *Reading for Self-Education*

The self-made man of letters is generally more influenced by his reading—random, as it may be—than is his more traditionally educated counterpart. And so with John Neal who read widely and deeply, but read to seize those ideas that confirmed his own prejudices and opinions. Because he lacked the experience of high school and college, he was thrown inward upon himself, and compelled to trust his own ideas rather than those of a received standard of knowledge. Aware of the liabilities of self-education, he also saw the asset of independent thought:

> The best-educated man is, after all, more self-educated than he is any thing else. . . . But to brag that you have made your way without the help of a collegiate course, what is it, after all, but an admission that a collegiate course has its advantages? And so it has; but look at the disadvantages. You grow to a mould; you adopt the opinions of your teacher. . . . (WR, 104)

Lacking formal teachers after the age of twelve, Neal nevertheless grew up in a teacher's family, and from the memory of his father and the example of his mother he early established the habit of reading widely and eagerly. As Elizabeth Oakes Smith recalled from attending Madam Neal's elementary school, ". . . it was a sort of patent of nobility to be a pupil to Madam Neal. She was a large, tall, handsome woman; of a fine presence, clear intellect, and no little self-reliance and independence of will."[12] Elsewhere Mrs. Smith refers to the inspiration toward reading that she received from Neal's mother; and certainly the twins John and Rachel received some of the same inspiration and self-reliance from their widowed mother who taught them the three R's before they entered public school.

Neal began his serious reading[13] when he was about eight. A neighbor lady with the delightful name of Thankful Bagley was baby-sitting for the active boy and offered him a copy of *Arabian Nights* with which to occupy himself. The young Neal took the volume off to the quiet of the attic and there spent the entire day in flights of fancy. The supper hour had passed when his mother found him at his favorite reading spot, the small attic window where he could curl up against a trunk and read a day away (WR, 109). His love of reading, already whetted on children's books and on the Bible, reached a new keenness with his exposure to the world of romance and imagination. Ahead lay the universe of literature and with it self-education.

At age ten John was reading voraciously whatever came to hand. His father's library included Young's *Night Thoughts, Robinson Crusoe, Tom Jones,* Thomas à Kempis, and *Charlotte Temple (WR,* 93). In addition, the boy trundled home old newspapers and magazines, stored them in his beloved attic, and there pored over them. Mrs. Smith remembers him at about this time as tall for his age, "striking in appearance; full of life and activity . . . apt to learn, tenacious in memory, always a little in excess in every way. . . ."[14] At this time, he struck up a lucky friendship with a slightly older boy who worked in one of Portland's lending libraries.[15] For a boy who had no spare cash for books, here was opportunity, for he was given the run of the library kept by Thomas Clark in Fish (now Exchange) Street. Clark had first advertised his New Circulating Library and bookstore in the *Eastern Argus* of September 15, 1803. Hours were "Early morning to 9 P.M." By 1805 he had increased his library from "4 to 16 hundred volumes" by buying out his older rival Adams. Clark now claimed his library to be the "only one in Portland." Monthly rates were seventy-five cents for subscribers or four to twelve cents per week depending upon the size of the borrowed book. In 1806 he was advertising the arrival of new "romances, novels, plays," and he was doing a thriving business supplying books on long term loan to masters of vessels plying out of the busy port.

Clark's treasures were open to Neal, who paid by running errands. He read his way through what was largely a collection of fiction, firing his young brain with Charles Brockden Brown—about the only American represented—and his British gothic predecessors, Mrs. Ann Radcliffe and William Godwin. Eighteenth century novelists included Jonathan Swift, Henry Fielding, Tobias Smollett, and Oliver Goldsmith, whose *Vicar of Wakefield* Neal admired all his life as one of the finest novels. From the Continent there were *Don Quixote* and St. Pierre's *Paul and Virginia.* Neal also read at this time Cook's *Voyages* and Rollin's *Ancient History.* He read, in short, what was available—travel, history, standard novels, and gothic romances.

When he reached Baltimore a decade later he was soon reading contemporary literature, the heady romantic writings of Lord Byron, Percy Bysshe Shelley (whose "Revolt of Islam" he read aloud to John Pierpont), Leigh Hunt, Thomas Moore, Thomas Campbell, and Charles Maturin. Of American writers, he grew familiar with Charles Dana, Joseph Dennie, Timothy Dwight, Benjamin Franklin, Washington Irving, James Kirke Paulding, Charles Sprague, and William Wirt as well as a host of now forgotten scribblers.

Through his passionate reading of fiction, Neal had developed skills of speed and retention that were to help him in his reading of the law. Not only had he developed a skill but also a theory of efficient reading. He advocated neither reading so slowly as to "lose the spirit of the author" nor so fast as to merely skim. Rather, he deliberately expanded the width of his focussed eye span, thus reducing the number of eye movements required per line. As he put it, "As I began with reading letter by letter, so I went on, reading syllables, then words, and at last whole phrases at a glance, until I had acquired a facility in serious reading, only to be matched by that of the most thorough-going novel-reader" (WR, 166). He was thus able to read and retain three hundred pages of law a day without fatigue. He had always been able to read without subvocalization.

To this skill in reading, he added a quick and eager mind, and he would have taken greater advantage of the educational opportunities of his boyhood city had family finances allowed. For example, the city offered good training in foreign languages—particularly French and Italian, which were offered by private emigré masters including those who developed Longfellow's linguistic facility. But the extra cost was beyond the means of Neal. Only when he was twenty-five did he draw on Yankee ingenuity to undertake "the study of French in a way of my own." By his method he learned to speak and write French, Spanish, Italian, and German, and to read Portuguese, and Swedish, besides classical Hebrew, Latin, Greek, and Anglo-Saxon (WR, 112). The essence of the method was to learn the pronunciation and then to dive into the reading of a book with the help of a dictionary, building toward adequate speed as he proceeded.

And thus, Neal summarized, ". . . I managed to educate myself, and without help from any living teacher" (WR, 104); that is, after age twelve when his formal schooling ended. Perhaps with a touch of self-justification, but also with more than a grain of truth, he looked back over his life and was glad that self-education had not molded his originality into someone else's shape.

In maturity, he always stood ready to offer aid to those who were seeking an education. When a group of young men were forming the Union Social Library in early 1829, Neal was among the men of the town who donated books to start the library; he gave eight volumes, including the *Spectator*, August von Kotzebue's *Anecdotes*, and *The Man of the World*.[16] As editor, he used his columns for educational purposes. He shared with his age an obsessive interest in correct grammar and right spelling, although his experience with formal grammar was not a happy or particularly rewarding one. He complained—like each generation down to the present—that he no sooner learned the system according to one text, than a new system was introduced "and I had to begin afresh and learn a new set of rules, with examples and exceptions, and the exceptions to exceptions, till I had got completely bewildered. . . . So that I have come to look upon English grammar as a delusion and a snare" (WR, 106–7). He continued to feel that grammars had use only as reference tools and certainly were not to be learned by heart, as was the custom in "grammar school." The stress on memorized rules and parsing of sentences did not teach correct or effective writing, which, he held sanely, was like horsemanship, best learned by doing. This strongly held opinion, however, did not keep him from acting as critic. The pages of the *Yankee* often carry his lists of errors detected in the writing and speaking of contemporaries. In an article on "Orthography," for example, he listed as commonly misspelled words "unpolite" for "impolite," "twaddle" for "twattle," "Dutchess," "alledge," and other phonetic failings. Like Poe, Neal never outgrew the practice of pillorying authors for alleged mistakes of spelling and grammar. In this the Americans were like their British counterparts, the editors John Lockhart and Edward Bulwer, who established their own impeccability by attack on the illeducation of those they reviewed. Neal's introduction to literary journalism was to come, not in Portland however, but in Baltimore.

III   *Club Life of Jehu O'Cataract*

In the spring of 1814 the young Neal took the stagecoach south from Portland, prompted by "a prodigious hankering not to die a fool; an event that inevitably happens to a New Englander who dies without seeing Boston." The same lure of expanding horizons led him on to New York and ultimately to Baltimore where he sought his fortune. At that time Baltimore was the third largest commercial city in the new nation, and there Neal hoped to prosper in the dry goods business. The end of the war, however, brought disaster, bankruptcy that jailed for a short time his partner and closest friend John Pierpont, and left Neal destitute. Out of the wreckage he determined to embark on joint careers of literature and law. Necessity was, of course, a strong spur to his literary resolve; but a deeper cause was the stimulus to his active mind of the society he found in the city.

Neal worked best under the excitement of exchange of ideas within a circle of friends. This opportunity he found in the Delphian Club of Baltimore,[17] and he was to find a similar excitement among the young men in Jeremy Bentham's household in London, and to a lesser extent in the literary group in Portland before 1836. Neal was what Dr. Johnson would have termed a clubable man, and he blossomed in the Delphian environment.

In the Baltimore that was emerging from the War of 1812, a group of high-spirited men were drawn together under the leadership of Dr. Tobias Watkins, a tall, handsome physician with a flair for paradox and wit. Pierpont, austere in looks but an irrepressible punster, and Neal, fiery and eager to make his mark, joined Watkins in founding on August 31, 1816, a small group, later limited to nine—"we being the male muses of our day!" recalled Neal. The ninth place was filled variously with a visiting Britisher and others. The regulars included Paul Allen, editor and writer who was squandering his talent in sluggishly performed hackwork; Henry M. Brackenridge, lawyer son of the famous novelist Hugh Henry Brackenridge and himself the author of a travel book, *Views of Louisiana* (1817); and William Gwynne, also a lawyer as well as editor of the *Federal Gazette*. The number of these litterateurs was rounded out by a German Dr. Readel who acted as secretary, and General William H. Winder, a leader of the Baltimore bar in whose office Neal was to read law. Winder was brilliant but was currently living down the American defeat at Bladensburg where the militia he commanded had failed to stop the British in their attack upon Washington.

Such was the group that met each Saturday night to eat cheese, drink beer, read papers, and discuss assigned topics. Each had wit, a love of fun and argumentation, and a mind that ranged over the terrain of American life and letters. This club life was in some ways a last flowering of eighteenth-century attitudes, as each member was given a "clubicular" name; Watkins, the president, was Pertinax Particular because of his natural spirit of contradiction; the learned Yale graduate John Pierpont was Hiero Heptaglott; and Neal in his Gaelic impetuosity was dubbed Jehu O'Cataract. As the Delphian Club the group soon founded a publication hopefully to rival Philadelphia's *Port Folio*. It was this periodical, *The Portico*, in which Neal first tasted the heady wine of literary success. The club itself provided a kind of advanced schooling for Neal, who alone of the group was self-educated. Among these professionals, he was stimulated to his first hectic but often brilliant efforts.

In the last six months of 1816, the bankrupt merchant of twenty-three burst into literature through the pages of *The Portico*. That year he was represented by eight poems, with such romantically revealing titles as "To Genius," "Moonlight," and "The Lyre of the Winds," interspersed by a four-part critical study of Lord Byron whose work strongly influenced the young Neal. During the first half of the following year the number of poems nearly doubled to fourteen, including a "Fragment in Imitation of Byron." Neal's "Song: The Sailor's Pledge,—By the friend of ———, who fell with Lawrence" was given special prominence as the final selection of the volume. His prose contributions revealed a number of his future interests. His essay on duelling was a foreshadowing of its treatment in *Keep Cool*, published the following year; his review of a life of Benjamin West and an essay on painters launched his early art criticism; and reviews of Maturin, of *Childe Harold's Pilgrimage, Canto 3*, and of a home-state poet's *The Village* began his poetic criticism and first sketching of his own literary theories.

Through the second half of 1817 Neal's poetic output remained high with nine poems, including a verse parody of the simplistic and moralizing newspaper poems of the day. In prose he contributed a review of *Manfred* as well as of Scott's *Tales of my Landlord*. But by 1818 Neal was turning increasingly to prose—both in the publication of his first novel and in his contributions to *The Portico*. These latter include no poems, but a number of critical articles, a sketch of Baltimore, and a review of *Childe Harold's Pilgrimage, Canto 4*. His interest in Byron was unabated; for he wrote "Our only wish was to make him, whom we consider the first of poets, better known in our country. . . ."[18] Broader interests are reflected in an article "What is the chief excellence of Shakespeare?" and in a philosophical study entitled "Man not a free agent." These had originally been written for the Delphian Club.

A format for the weekly meetings of the Delphians (which Neal was to introduce to the young men of Portland in 1829)[19] included essays on assigned topics. Usually set by the president, Tobias Watkins, three topics were presented to the group before being bound in the record book, and—at least the best—published in *The Portico*. For two years Neal averaged an essay about every two weeks, several times ingeniously weaving all three topics into a single essay. Neal's choice of topics, as Richards[20] has noted, reveals interests that were to remain with the young author throughout his career. Typical are the following:

"Wherein is a man disgraced who refused to accept a challenge to fight a duel?" (January 4, 1817). This is a central theme in *Keep Cool.*

"By which of the Arts can the productions of Nature be more completely represented, Painting or Sculpture?" (September 27, 1817). Here is the germ of Neal's interest in the relationship of the arts.

"Seeing that extremes run into each other, what is the difference between vice and virtue?" (November 15, 1817). Neal's demonic heroes are hero/ villains in the Brockden Brown tradition.

"What constitutes the essential difference between Poetry and Prose?" (January 10, 1818). His answer (as printed in *Portico* 2.214): "We think that poetry is as much the power of saying in verse what cannot be said in prose, as it is any thing else."

"What are the anomalies, the principal ones, in the English Law?" (July 3, 1819). The answers are developed dramatically in the trial scene of *Rachel Dyer.*

To the set question of June 13, 1818, *What is the chief excellence of Shakespeare?* Neal answered promptly " . . . his simplicity, his artlessness those unaffected touches of natural eloquence, in which the man only is heard. . . ." That is, Shakespeare for the romantic Neal is great because his native talent pours unadorned from his heart.

In 1818 Neal himself was still practicing the "natural eloquence" of poetry; the year was to see the publication by the Portico press of his ambitious long poems. The volume in paper wrappers carried a title page of *Battle of Niagara. A poem, without notes; and Goldau, or The Maniac Harper. "Eagles! and Stars! and Rainbows!" By Jehu O'Cataract, Author of Keep Cool, &c.* The insistence on no notes was his follow-up on a point he made the year before in reviewing Enoch Lincoln's poem *The Village;* he had then regretted Lincoln's inclusion of prose notes as a slavish copying of European models. The pseudonym of Jehu O'Cataract was a public introduction of his name within the Delphian Club; for his rash outpouring of words, written or delivered at white heat and without revision, he was known to overflow in word or print like a cataract with no more restraint than the biblical Jehu. The fitness of the name assured that it stuck by him, to haunt him as an echoing refrain by reviewers long after he wished to discontinue the myth of his hurried and unrevised composition.[21]

In these early years, however, Neal himself contributed to the misconception that he wrote with unnecessary haste. In a note in *Blackwood's* he boasted how he had written *Randolph* in thirty-six days, *Errata* in less than thirty-nine, and *Seventy-Six* in twenty-seven, all while engaged in professional business. And there is a good deal of truth in the way in which he drove himself in those Baltimore days when he was studying law and storming the literary scene in attempts to recoup his lost fortunes. As reported by Rufus Griswold, in his *Poets and Poetry of America,*

When he [Neal] lived in Baltimore, . . . [he] went one evening to the rooms of Pierpont, and read him a poem which he had just completed. [When some faults were pointed out,] Neal promised to revise it, and submit it again on the following morning. At the appointed time he repaired to the apartment of his friend, and read to him a new poem, of three or four hundred lines. He had tried to improve the first, but failing to do so, had chosen a new subject, a new measure, and produced an entirely new work, before retiring to bed.[22]

Impatient by nature, Neal spurned the drudgery and self-criticism that revision demanded, bolstering his natural inclination with a doctrine of composition that gave highest value to romantic, nearly automatic writing. Jehu O'Cataract preferred to burst upon the page with all the sins of first draft about him rather than incurring the risk of deadening the emotional impact by letting the intellect correct the product.

In developing his aesthetic, Neal had faulted the pale neoclassical poem of Enoch Lincoln as being highly respectable: "It does not exhibit so much of what a fine imagination would call *poetry*, as of that old fashioned and almost obsolete quality, which we denominate meaning. . . ."[23] Such tameness could not be charged against the poems in Neal's volume. Even in the short poem "Expression" extolling the beauty of dark eyes over tame blue eyes, his imagery reaches after effects of the sublime, as he concludes: "The other, the foam of the cataract's dash, / The darker the water, the brighter the flash."

The cataract's dash was also central to the title poem "Battle of Niagara," eighty pages of heroic couplets on an American subject; "I have attempted to do justice to American scenery and American character, not to versify the minutiae of battles. . . ," he wrote in his introduction, and asks the reader to "remember, I have not attempted to write a *history*, but a *poem*." The time was ripe for such an attempt and the popular reception—while lagging behind that accorded Pierpont's *Airs of Palestine*—was such as to warrant in 1819 a second edition, augmented by some of the shorter poems that had appeared in *The Portico*, for example "The Lyre of the Winds," the hymn he wrote for the ordination of Pierpont, and the first book of a projected blank verse epic on "The Conquest of Peru."

These were the years of Neal's first and strongest Byronism, although his novels were never to be free of the titanic type of hero spawned by the English poet. Under the spell of Byron's *Manfred*, which he had discovered while preparing his articles on Byron for *The Portico*, and of the work of Maturin, especially *Bertram*, which he saw acted by the tragedian Thomas Cooper, Neal dashed off a verse drama *Otho* in 1819.[24] In his preface, Neal worries about the extent of his imitation of these European models, although he admits that he fashioned his hero on Bertram so that the role might appeal to Cooper as another vehicle for his special talents. In a review in *The Portico* he had praised Cooper as well as the Maturin play, which he preferred to *Manfred* for its better morality, for Byron tends to "blind us to the guilt of incest."[25] He was still of the same mind years later when he accepted Mrs. Stowe's vindication of Lady Byron, recalling how as young poet, he had "enthroned him [Byron] above the stars; but as a man . . . I regarded him as a sort of melo-dramatic personage turned adrift upon the world, as if out of Astley's amphitheatre."[26]

When *Otho* failed to interest the actor Cooper, Neal still had hopes for eventual production, for he carried it with him to England to seek at least publication there. Even when revised, however, *Otho*[27] was more rhetorical than poetic and too rantingly obscure; the plot was at once both mystifying and trite. The hero's desperation fails of the "terrible sublimity" that Neal sought. Surprisingly, the play observes the unities, in order, writes Neal in his preface, to aid the audience in their "acquiescence" to the fiction. Since the audience do not believe that the characters are the people they represent, the writer must "carry them away," "confounding two distinct operations of the mind—acquiescence and belief." The dramatist must do nothing "to dispel the little delusion—the acquiescence of the mind." This theory, reminiscent of Coleridge's willing suspension of disbelief, unfortunately does not work in Neal's actual practice, although his dependence on the unities was so defended.[28]

Clearly Neal's outburst of poetry during these years was stimulated by the society of Baltimore as well as by his personal ferment and his study of Byron. Writing his autobiography at the advanced age of seventy-six, he recalled vividly the Baltimore circle and devoted a disproportionate amount of space to recounting his poetry of those years. Aside from a political essay in the Hallowell *Gazette*, he had

not written for publication until in Baltimore "having become acquainted with a set of handsome, clever, and very pleasant young
women, with something of a literary taste, it was proposed by one of
their number, a Miss Maria C., to form a club, and furnish weekly,
each in turn, a paper upon any subject we chose. . . ."[29] From this
impetus came his prose sketches such as "Thoughts on Female
Impropriety" in the short-lived *Wanderer* and the prose and poetry of
The Portico.

Thus launched, Neal found a kindred interest and a friendly critic
in his partner John Pierpont who was writing and polishing his *Airs of
Palestine,* the success of which upon publication in 1816 further
prodded Neal to competition. But, whereas Pierpont labored with
classic restraint, Neal, as he put it, "began to seethe and simmer," for
"mine was a clear case of spontaneous combustion."[30] Pierpont
provided the tinder for Neal's conflagration when he suggested the
subjects of both "Goldau" and "Niagara." Reading aloud a passage
from a travel book about the destruction of an Alpine Village,
Pierpont suggested it as a "capital subject for a poem; and you are the
very boy to do it into English verse." Neal caught fire and within a
couple of days had completed his "red-hot thunderbolts."[31]

Likewise the subject of a battle near the great falls of Niagara was
Pierpont's suggestion. Over the years, the two friends dreamed of a
joint trip to this American wonder which, with the Natural Bridge of
Virginia, was described in its sublimity by every romantic traveler.
His head filled with the vigor of Byron, Neal responded to the idea of
the thundering waters, although he was not to see them until years
later.[32]

By the time Neal's two long poems were published, Pierpont had
already left Baltimore for theological studies in Cambridge. The
publication took him by surprise, but his response was quick and his
praise, lavish. In a letter to his wife, which he shared with Neal, he
wrote

The poems are both very great, admirable, astonishing, indeed. He has
thrown his whole character into them; and either of them contains more of
the greatness and madness of poetry than *any* other poem that was ever
written in America. True, they have great defects, of which I think their not
unfrequent obscurities are the most conspicuous. But all the defects are more
than a thousand times counterbalanced by the beauties.

. . . the poetry is better, more grand, sublime, and original than any other
American poetry. The "Airs of Palestine," as a whole poem, is more correct,

and more harmonious; more polished in the structure of the verse, but immeasurably more *tame.*

In thus comparing his own *Airs* with his friend's work, Pierpont decided, indeed, to give up poetry—holding to the decision for twenty years, since "what with him was labor, to me [Neal] was mere play," reports Neal.[33]

IV A Romantic Aesthetic

The madness, sublimity, and even obscurity which Pierpont noted in the poems was the result of Neal's romantic aesthetic. While he would later expand and clarify his views of poetry, by 1818 Neal's basic tenets were already established.[34] True poetry, he believed, arises from passion: "It is the part of genuine poetry to furnish a clue to the labyrinths of passion. . . . Poetry is the lightning of intuition—every object is brightened into importance by its flash."[35] When gripped by sufficient emotion, all men will naturally rise to poetry which is, he contends, a "natural musick" and the very language of the human heart.[36] This romantic linking of the various arts through a quest for their common sources and common effects was later elaborated by Neal: "Music itself is but one kind of poetry, eloquence another. Indeed it were safe to say that Music and Painting, and Eloquence, and Sculpture, and Architecture, and Poetry, are but different manifestations of the same power— interchangeable terms."[37] In a seminal essay, Benjamin Lease[38] has demonstrated that, beneath the seemingly scattered and random remarks, lies a unified theory of literature that remained remarkably constant throughout Neal's long life. While he was following one of the main streams of European romanticism, he was pioneering the ideas in the America of 1820. Expounding the then current psychology, he distinguished three faculties of man: brain, blood, and heart. Only the latter two are for Neal "natural," for brain is the product of artificial effort and skill. Brain—intellect and reason—should in poetry and fiction occur only when fused with blood and heart, when living thought occurs without the order imposed by logic and syllogistic reasoning. Especially under emotional stress, logic goes down before chaotic vitality. Brain-writing, then, for Neal is something other than true literature. Rather, the literature of blood and heart will neither build upon nor appeal to artificial skills but will evoke varied emotional responses in the reader by varied literary stimuli. In particular, the blood is aroused by the sublime, by that which is mysterious, grandiose, indistinct, awesome. The heart is touched by sympathy with the manifestations of another human heart. The poet of the blood will deal with the mystery of angels and spirits, with the human subservient to the supernatural; mystery, commotion, and indefiniteness will be heightened with a concurrent avoidance of clarity, repose, and completeness; the language will be magniloquent, metaphorical, filled with allusion and hyperbole. To such stimuli, the reader will respond involuntarily and spontaneously. But the terrific impact of the effect cannot be sustained by the reader for a lengthy period, and thus the poem itself should not be overly long. Poets of the blood would be Byron, Neal himself, and Poe, whose pronouncements on the essential brevity of true poetry was to become a commonplace.

Poetry of the heart differs from poetry of the blood in needing to seek means to build an emotional rapport with the link which fuses the hearts of men when they respond to genuine emotion in others. Here artifice and drama are fatal to the effect; only the simple action of a fellow human being in and of itself speaks to the reader's sympathy. Accordingly, the poet of the heart deals with the homely, simple, and familiar. His language will be natural, the dialogue striving to reflect actual speech in a natural setting so that both may augment character. As an example Neal points to Thomas Moore, whom he contrasts to Byron; but Wordsworth, Whittier, and later Whitman might be added as exemplars.

Neal further realizes that point of view is vital to literary effects, especially as they try to appeal to the heart. In an age generally committed to the omniscient author point of view, he argues for one restricted to a single central character, the one channel through which the reader's affinity may flow. All information not known to this central character, then, is to be withheld from the reader.

Some appreciation of this literary theory of Neal's is essential to an understanding of his work. The thundering poetry with its appeal to blood; the novels with their central Byronic heroes, their experimentation with "talking on paper," and their use of dialect and local detail emerge as conscious attempts to illustrate and further a unified theory of literature. When so seen, it is possible to understand the basis for Poe's evaluation of Neal as "first, or at all events second among our men of indisputable *genius*," a man endowed with a "philosophical and self-dependent spirit which has always distinguished him. . . ."[39]

Connections with Poe have been explored by J. J. Rubin,[40] who points out that Neal's essay "What is Poetry?" appeared in *Sartain's Union Magazine* in 1849 just one month before Poe's posthumous "Poetic Principle." Rubin also detects a possible influence on Whitman, noting Neal's call to American writers in his *Down-Easters* to employ the "American language," and his insistence that poetry is always poetry even if printed as prose.[41] Furthermore, about a year after Whitman ceased to edit the New York *Aurora* there appeared in its pages an article by Neal insisting on the universality of the poetic impulse and providing examples that foreshadow Whitman's own practice.

Just as Byron provided the model for Neal's poetic work, so A. W. Schlegel provided the central impetus to Neal's developing literary theory. The recently translated *Course of Lectures on Dramatic Art and Literature*[42] was the subject of debate among the Delphians. Their local interest in Schlegel's doctrine of effect was further supported by the enthusiasm of J. G. Lockhart when he became associated with *Blackwood's* in 1817, for this journal was quickly read when it arrived in Baltimore. Here in Schlegel was the common source for Neal's and Poe's literary theories.[43]

Judged by time, Neal's own poetic practice was less successful, however, than either his editorial encouragement of others or his critical pronouncements. Yet in these activities he spoke with the strength of a practitioner, as he himself insisted any critic should: "To *judge* of poetry, or of any thing, indeed," he has a fictional mouthpiece say, "a man should be a *workman*, at the same trade."[44] Neal's later career as editor and critic, then, rests on his own poetic practice when he burst forth in Baltimore. True, the sublimity of *Goldau's* Alpine catastrophe no longer appeals, the tired Miltonic diction of the unfinished epic *The Conquest of Peru* was never fresh, and much that Neal (and his contemporaries) considered poetry was a kind of shouting rhetoric. For example, his once-popular "Shakespeare's Tomb" opens

> Rash man! Forbear!
> Thou wilt not surely tread
> On the annointed head
> Of him that slumbereth there!

Vigor and rhetorical apostrophe it has; but none of the freshness of diction or image that mark fine poetry.

But not all is contemptible. Neal's "Birth of a Poet"[45] has some memorable lines, and "The Marriage Ring"[46] has at least one effective stanza. As a whole, the latter poem is marred by graveyard sentimentality ("For she had felt the lips of *death*/Pressed to her golden marriage-ring!"), but earlier in the poem, as the dying sister takes farewell of the bride, occurs a quatrain that reminds one of the later macabre effects of Poe:

> And saying this, her light frame shook
> And all her black redundant hair
> Broke loose, and like a shadow fell
> Upon the snowy pillow there.

As a poet, Neal wished to be remembered for his "Niagara." But even this most ambitious of his poems is flawed by a diction too repetitive of outworn "plumes," "furl'd banners," and "seraphs," of contractions ("ne'er," "o'er"), of "yon" this and "yon" that, and compound epithets ("sun-shiny vests," "lustre-crown'd peaks," "blue-bosom'd water"). Insufficient to save the poem is the occasionally striking image: the sound of the cavalcade at sunset is ". . . as cheerful and wild/As the echo of caves to the laugh of a child." Or again, the solitude of the lake was not meant to reflect horrors of war and fear: instead, "Ontario's deeps are spread to multiply/But sunshine, stars, the moon, and clear-blue sky." A section dealing with movements of the troops at night evokes a ghostly foreboding of the impending death of the cavalry: "Their heads muffled up to their white filmy eyes." And in describing the morning after battle, he captures the carnage by focussing on the riderless horses and the soldier who is unimpressed by the many slaughtered men until death is numbered in one:

> And only, when he meets a comrade there,
> Stretch'd calmly out, with brow and bosom bare,
> And stiffen'd hand uplifted in the air—
> With lip still curl'd, and open, glassy eye,
> Fix'd on the pageant that is passing by—
> And only then—in decency will ride
> Less stately in his strength, less lordly in his pride.

Touches of the poet are surely there, but the couplets of "Niagara" tumble on until the reader tires of a Scott-like gallop that lacks Scott's clarity and vividness. All in all, Neal's theory is more exciting than his practice, and his lesser poems appeal more than his grandly conceived "Niagara."

Like his friend Longfellow, he had grown up in a ballad-loving and ballad-producing town.[47] The modern reader would wish more of such rhythmical ballads as Neal's "Cape Cottage":

> Hurrah for Cape Cottage, hurrah!
>   Hurrah for the sight of the sea!
> Hurrah for the girls that are found there!
> Hurrah for the rocks that abound there!
> With perch weighing more than a pound there!
>   Hurrah for the wind blowing free.

Yet this is the judgment of another time. To his contemporaries, Neal's poetry was evoked in one of twelve "Poetical Portraits of Prominent Portland Poets":

> The mighty cataract's thunderous roar—
>   The sweep of eagle's wings—
> And tramp of armies on their march,
>   With him are sacred things.[48]

The images are all from "Niagara," which had carried the motto on its title page of "Eagles! and Stars! and Rainbows!"[49] To mid-nineteenth-century readers, John Neal was ever Jehu O'Cataract, the poet of "Niagara."

CHAPTER 2

Experiments in American Fiction

I N an eight year period John Neal published six novels,[1] each in many ways unpolished and hectic but each an experiment in treating American themes and scenes in an American way. That they were written with what Neal called "marvellous rapidity" and what critics damned as "fatal facility" is attested by the author himself; indeed he wishes to astound with his boast:

> *Keep Cool* was "written in hot weather" in 1816.
> *Logan* . . . I wrote in six or eight weeks, ending Nov. 17, 1821;
> *Randolph*, I began Nov. 26, 1821, and finished in thirty-six days;
> *Errata* . . . was begun Jan. 8, 1822, and finished in thirty-nine days;
> *Seventy-Six,* begun Feb. 16, 1822, and finished March 19, 1822—four days off—in twenty-seven days.[2]

All this feverish writing was while Neal was pursuing his law studies, and writing for the press. Only *Brother Jonathan* (1825), which he took in manuscript to England and there rewrote for *Blackwood's*, escapes his boast of speed. Actually the first as well as the last of this series of early novels was fully revised, yet these two are no better for it than the others. In fact, *Seventy-Six* is without doubt the best, despite its having been struck off in a month.

Neal's pride in speedy composition was intended as a boast. He was more than a little a showman, trained in his apprentice years to the sharp come-on of salesmanship. As he sets out to sell his writing, he is advertising himself as a rash and fiery genius. Perhaps he oversold his image, although there is scant evidence that he could have done better with more leisure. A touch of genius he had, but to the end it remained undisciplined and unchanneled.

I Keep Cool

At twenty-three, Neal was struggling to support himself while reading for the law, and although stimulated by the publication of his poems and articles in *The Portico*, he had received no money for these contributions. As he put it, "I now began to cast about for something better to do—something, at least, that would pay better; and, after considering the matter for ten minutes or so, determined to try my hand at a novel" (*WR*, 196). Even then Neal was so constituted as to throw himself wholeheartedly into nearly hopeless causes. To make a living by writing was such a cause, for by this summer of 1816 fewer than seventy novels by Americans had been published and fewer still had been a financial success. There were the examples of Charles Brockden Brown's series of hurried novels, of Brackenridge's *Modern Chivalry*, and of Royall Tyler's *The Algerine Captive:* otherwise the field of fiction in America lay in the genteel hands of the women who wrote sentimental novels of seduction. To expect to increase his income by writing a novel was as unrealistic as it was typical of Neal.

But a novel it was to be; he proceeded to write in a fine frenzy, stating "I shall write as others drink, for exhilaration"[3]. The resulting outpouring was novel indeed, with its mock-serious title "Judge Not from First Appearances." The manuscript was entrusted to his friend Pierpont, by now in Massachusetts studying for the ministry, who sought without success among the Boston publishers for someone to buy the book (*WR*, 196–97). In rejecting it, they found the women too earthy, too susceptible to male overtures,[4] while lacking the higher flights of love: "There is not quite *love* enough in it to suit the ladies," was the judgment of Mrs. Read, wife of one of the publishers with whom Pierpont shared the manuscript. Neal accepted the criticism—tamely for him—and set about rewriting the work with a new title of *Keep Cool*. Another friend, Dr. Watkins, interested the Baltimore publisher Joseph Cushing in taking the toned-down version. Neal jumped at the offer of two hundred dollars "like a cock at a gooseberry" (*WR*, 197), but whether Neal had tamed his wild genius and outspoken Yankee realism sufficiently for the lady readers is, however, questionable.

In an age used to Richardsonian heroines of sentiment, Neal's women are too pert. Harriet teases the hero: "I can put you in good humor any time, by a little *flattery*, no matter how gross" (*KC*, I, 41). Treading on still more dangerous ground, she can fall in a faint in the hero's arms, only to revive enough to saucily admonish him to "keep cool" (*KC*, I, 40). Fainting, after all, confides the author, is "the last and highest of their witcheries, and the next after hysterics and tears." Such puncturing of the facade of female decorum could not be offset by Neal's dedication: "To his Country Women the Author, who is an American, respectfully dedicates this work." Neal does, however, defend American womanhood from the coquettry of Laura by having her born abroad albeit by American parents. She has become "Italianate." Her behavior is revealed as play-acting when, to be entertaining, she mimics her friends to perfection. The scene foreshadows by almost thirty years the similar unmasking of Major Bulstrode in Cooper's *Satanstoe*. The open honesty of Americans can see through the sophisticated role-playing of the European.

In spite of this patriotic bias, the book still had for novel readers of the day too many characters who relish their sins, and to them the author gave the best lines: the rakish Charles Percy likes all women, for "his mother and his sister were women, and he could have hugged to his heart all that resembled them. . . ." Further "Charles had the heart of a man; when he saw perfection—and every thing young and lovely seemed to him to be perfection—he worshipped it. . ." (*KC*, I, 25). Unfortunately, Charles also likes to tell of his adventures with women, a trait he shares with later Neal characters. He has in Laura a female counterpart who is allowed her defense of fickleness and flirtation: "Who can answer for the constancy of woman? Besides . . . it is not I who change, but the *object*" (*KC*, I, 172).

Neal was enjoying himself in this novel, enjoying being a bit outrageous, projecting his own O'Cataract character into the story, and writing with an eye on the ladies of the Baltimore circle who had first led him into literature. As a bachelor—by choice or the exegencies of bankruptcy—he was at the time of writing his first novel teasing his married friend Pierpont and boasting of the superior ability of an unmarried man to start, as they were doing, a new career: he wrote, "You are at that age when such misfortunes are most terrible—the sapling may be prostrated with little damage to the oak itself—but when the oak falls, a thousand dependences fall with it."[5] There is as much self-justification as gratuitous moralizing in such remarks to his friend; and there is certainly a young man's self-justification as well as crypto-confession in his treatment of the romantic tendencies of his fictional characters.

So also there is self-advertisement when he reprints his *Portico* poems "To Genius" and "To Fancy" as illustrations of a discussion of poetry (*KC*, I, 124–31), or when he argues that every author publishes because he has a high opinion of himself—and hence should not play at false modesty (*KC*, I, 114–15). Yet in the preface his boasts are tempered with coyness as he admits that for all its faults, the book is the best that the author can make it. In fact, the reader is constantly warned from title to introductory words at chapter openings, to "Keep Cool."

The result of this self-conscious playfulness is an ambiguity of tone. As much as anything, the shifting of tone from arch attempts at wit through mock seriousness to concern for social issues confuses the reader, who indeed must keep cool if he is not to lose all patience. As a first novel, *Keep Cool* is too rich a pudding; individual plums can be savored only when abstracted from the seething mass. The strangely modern ring of Earnest's insult to his landlord—"Keep cool, daddy" (*KC*, I, 61)—is followed by a republican attack on the use of titles, even those of military rank (*KC*, I, 62–63). An accurate description of the varied crowd on a Hudson River boat[6] turns into frontier-type horseplay as the group convinces a luxuriously bewhiskered man to shave himself clean because whiskers have been found to induce facial cancer. By the time the reader is swept into the second volume, his head spins with new characters, such as the Byronic poet Echo,[7] and with social issues ranging from arguments against capital punishment to defenses of the noble Indian. Yet the narrative dramatizes an opposite view, as bloodthirsty Indians drawn from captivity narratives provide a "glorious" chase for the rescuers.

Keep Cool is a young man's novel, filled with too many diverse elements and episodes through which a racing prose tumbles the weary reader. It is embellished with coy humor such as its titular refrain and false chapter epigraphs,[8] and is often marred by brashness: "I have no respect for Aristotle; his criticism is fast following his philosophy" (*KC*, II, 126).

Faulty as it may be, the book has energy, and deserves more than the passing reference afforded it in standard studies of early American fiction. The preface helps to set it in historical perspective. Alluding to foreign attacks on American writing, Neal proclaims

The time will arrive, when the production of American science and genius, will bear some proportion to the scale of their inspiration. The time will arrive, when these slanders, and these aspersions will be forgotten; when our posterity will wonder that we could have ever doubted the everlasting charter of greatness that is written upon our barriers:—our cataracts—our rivers—and our mountains. (*KC*, I, xvi)

A great landscape will evoke a concomitantly great literature, boasts Neal in a fervor of literary nationalism built upon association psychology. And if *Keep Cool* fails of greatness, as it does, it is eminently American in its individuality that achieves eccentricity, in its brashness, in its flashes of earthiness puncturing pretension, and in its moral earnestness regarding social reform.

It was this last that Neal later claimed as his major purpose. In retrospect, after he had been made notorious for his antiduelling stance following the publication of *Randolph,* Neal increasingly felt that he had written his first novel in order to strike a blow as a social reformer: "In writing this story, I had two objects in view: one was to discourage duelling; and another was—I forget what" (*WR*, 197). But even here the playfulness of the last clause undercuts the seriousness of the first statement. If indeed *Keep Cool* had been planned as an antiduelling novel, he waited overly long to introduce the topic—195 pages. It is true that Neal had debated the duelling question before the Delphian Club and had published his thoughts in *The Portico.* As a young Quaker boy he had doubtless been impressed by the public outcry when Burr had killed Hamilton in 1804; there is little doubt of Neal's sincere abhorrence of the *code duello* as an aristocratic holdover inappropriate to the democratic scene. He held flatly that "duelling is the worst of murders" (*KC*, I, 209) and stressed the class element whereby "in America, a *gentleman* may cut another's throat, or blow out his brains with complete impunity. Here, the vulgar only are hanged for murder" (*KC*, I, 231).

But one senses less of the social reformer than the novelist in the work itself. The few early American novels that served Neal as models generally had a strong didactic strain, often as defense against those who held the genre immoral. Here as elsewhere Neal seems to be using the didactic mainly to illustrate the towering intellect of his titanic heroes. Cast in the mold of Manfred, his supermen must project intellectual power. Further, Neal is developing a Godwinian plot. Like Godwin's Caleb Williams, a good man who is goaded into a justified murder but is destroyed by the guilt that haunts him, Neal's Sydney is a Byronic English officer who is provoked into a duel with the lady's man Charles Percy. With his antagonist fatally wounded, Sydney flees civilization to do penance among the Indians by whom, it is revealed, he had formerly been adopted. Neal seems to have intended an exploration of the effects of guilt and expiation. But he loses himself as well as his hero in the murky woods, bringing him back to an un-Godwinian happy ending: Sydney and Laura kneel penitently before the portrait of Percy, marry, and produce cherubic twins.

Keep Cool is finally a confused and confusing book, but one that pioneers in the use of American material, including the Indian. In its attempts to deal with sin and expiation it intrigued the undergraduate Hawthorne. And, in what was then a predominantly feminine field (Cooper's *Pioneers* was six years in the future), Neal's novel is healthily masculine even in its faults. As a recent critic states, "Whatever objections may be raised against *Keep Cool* . . . the book can hardly be called monotonous."[9] The final judgment is Neal's: "The idea . . . was original enough . . . [but] there was much in it . . . that was boyish . . . " (*WR*, 221).

II Logan

Despite the cool reviews of his first novel, Neal was launched into prose. Like Pierpont he had vowed to give over poetry after the publication of his first volume, actually promising to write only in prose. The shift from his rhetorical poetry to poetic rhetoric was not a great one for him, and he supported his literary practice by his developing theory of poetry that was expanded to embrace a new prose-poetry. Some of his clearest statements were to appear in *Randolph*, but even before writing *Logan* he held that the literature of the future was to be heart literature in which "man must be the hero—and his heart the world which is convulsed in his career: the passions of man are the most terrible ministers—more terrible— infinitely more so, than the familiars of Milton's angel."[10] *Logan* presents in passionate prose such a hero.

Whereas his first novel had been rewritten out of deference to the lady reader, *Logan* was Neal unrestrained. He breaks violently from the genteel tradition that apologized for fiction as the product of an author's leisure hours, designed to improve the leisure hours of others by its good moral principles and exposure of vice.[11] Neal now proclaimed the novel as the very highest of literary forms. Just as he had broadened his concept of poetry to include all emotive language, he expanded the novel to include the best of all fiction, whether drama or verse, "where imaginary creatures, invested with all the attributes of humanity, agitated by the passions of our nature, are put to the task of entertaining or terrifying us."[12] Further, the novel, because it is read by people who never read anything else, is capable of greater influence than any other art form; it therefore calls to the man of greatest talent to provide the best possible novels. Men should enter a field that is too important to leave to "women and children," for "To write a good novel, a man should be a poet, a dramatist, a tragick and comick writer, a philosopher, a preacher, and an orator. . . ." (S, II, 228). In short, the novelist should be a John Neal, who setting flying pen to paper, poured his own passionate nature into *Logan*, his concept of a new novel for a new country.

At the time Neal had been managing to eke out a living from his writing. The two hundred dollars he received for *Keep Cool* had been followed by one hundred dollars worth of books for his volume of poetry and one hundred dollars for his drama *Otho*. Still desperate to support himself while he read the law, he engaged in the sheer drudgery—"sixteen hours a day, every day, including sabbaths . . . for four full months"—in indexing the first twelve volumes of *Niles' Weekly Register*. For this he received two hundred dollars plus the unexpected gift of a bound set of the *Register*, worth another one hundred dollars.[13] When a fellow Delphian, Paul Allen, was unable to fulfill a commitment for which subscriptions had already been sold, Tobias Watkins and John Neal teamed up to write Allen's *History of the American Revolution* (1819) on a payment per page basis. Neal hoped to do better with the more congenial work of his second novel.[14]

The resulting two volumes that burst upon the public in 1822 were, reflected Neal, a "wild, passionate, extravagant affair with some . . . of the most eloquent and fervid writing I was ever guilty of, either in prose or poetry" (WR, 223). Watkins, who received his copy in Washington, D.C., at once recognized O'Cataract's rhetoric in "every sentence, every line—nay, every thought, idea, phrase, expression." Somewhat ambiguously he concluded that *Logan* "is one of the most extraordinary productions of the present age . . . no other man on earth could have written such a book."[15] While no one knew just what to make of it, the book was a sensation, with readers taking it "as they took . . . exhilarating gas . . ." (WR, 224). Down to the present, critics have continued to have trouble dealing with this tale of American gothicism; Alexander Cowie states flatly, "*Logan* is not a nice story. Superstition, supernatural suggestions, brutality, sensuality, colossal hatred, delirium, rape, insanity, murder are the stuff out of which Neal weaves a Gothic tapestry never quite paralleled by Charles Brockden Brown or Poe."[16] Cowie forgot incest in his list of horrors.

Whereas Neal's first novel had ended among the Indians, *Logan* at the outset proclaims itself to be a truly American story by a native American, purportedly the last of the Mingos. Chapter 1 is in the form of a letter from the fictional narrator, written from exile in London at midnight on December 31, 1820. A second chapter leaves the epistolary device with its first person point of view to give a narrative review of the Virginia Indian Logan, a legendary chieftain who started as a friend of the whites but turned to vengeance after the massacre of his Indian wife and family. In actuality he is an Englishman gone renegade, begetting sons in wrath to carry on his vengeance before disappearing—à la King Arthur—leaving behind his mighty bow that none can draw. But unknown to Logan, his son Harold has survived the massacre and has been adopted by the governor. It is this son who is the central Byronic titan of the story. A word picture—*ut pictora poesis*—sketches his mother as an Indian queen in panther skin, sandaled feet, and carrying a bow; this dusky Diana is, however, no virgin huntress, for she is surrounded by naked children, a fruitful Eve of the forest.

With the background material behind him. Neal races into the story improper with Chapter 3. The gigantic Logan suddenly appears before the governor, who faints. The garrison is in a panic, but superhero Harold returns, assumes command, and restores order as Logan escapes with the Indian treaties. Harold goes on the warpath as an Indian killer, vying with Logan for the lovely Indian girl Loena. This father-son rivalry seems ended when Logan is reported to have wed Loena and started a new family. Meanwhile the governor's young wife, the Lady Elvira—a lively combination of pride and contrariness—harbors a secret passion for Logan whom she saw before her rescue by the governor from a massacre. Unconsciously in love with Harold as a surrogate for Logan, she ambiguously accepts his visit to her bedchamber.[17] The jealous governor banishes Harold to the forest where his parentage is revealed by an apparently mortally wounded Logan. Inheriting the feud to kill all whites, Harold also inherits Loena. As leader of the Indians, he runs amok in pillage and carnage, learning the uses of pain both as a protection of self and as a means of defining pleasure.

He becomes, however, a truly noble savage during his honeymoon idyll with Loena: "The moonlight shone upon their faces—they embraced, and slept, like two children, innocent and lonely, and helpless; without one impure thought, one throb of sensuality to disturb their beloved dreaming—*Their priest was solitude.*' "[18] In their forest Eden they rise to wed one another by starlight, and then "They knelt together: her warm cheek rested upon his, her dark tresses hung waving over her bosom. . . . Heart throbbed against heart; mouth breathed upon mouth; and their intertwining arms, in the pure innocence of their embrace, trembled at the same moment, with the same sensation" (*L*, I, 239). The scene, with its echoes of *Paradise Lost,* is one of the first to present the American Adam as wilderness lover, and it ends with the further Edenic touch of the beasts passing by and leaving the couple unmolested as they drift into innocent sleep. Less innocent perhaps was Neal's titillation of his readers with the physical warmth of a passage that reveals something of his own heated imagination. His dream woman is like his Bill Frazier's "woman as she is by nature, the Woman of the Woods, the exalted creature that issues uncorrupted, untouched from the hand of her Almighty Father! Eves of the great wilderness! Angels of solitude!"[19]

Harold's forest idyll ends as he travels to Quebec where the governor sends him to Europe to be trained as a proper leader of his people. Loena is left behind to be trained by the governor's wife. As he embarks, the first volume is rapidly coming to a close with Harold heroically rescuing a child who falls overboard at sea and repulsing a French boarding party. He and a lovely girl faint together, he of wounds, she of passion, as the reader is teased on to the sequel volume.

The plot, which for all its fervor in Volume 1 had been that of a border romance, now runs out of control. The widowed Elvira shows up on shipboard with her child Leopold, who proves to be Harold's contribution to their not so ambiguous night. Oscar, a second romantic genius, is also aboard and turns out to be Harold's brother as Loena is his sister. To the incest motif is added further murky sexuality when it is known that Oscar once wooed and won Elvira. The meaning of Neal's subtitle "A Family History" is fast becoming family fiasco. After discoursing eloquently on slavery, including the legal slavery of those under twenty-one, the apprentice and the indentured, Oscar leaps into the sea, a suicide expiating the murder of a woman he once slew at sea. The ocean crossing is further enlivened with gory scenes of two dead captains,[20] the hanging of pirates from the yardarm, and the passing of a slave ship; dead slaves wash by the ship, described with chilling details of fish-eaten bodies.

Harold is brought safely to England, where he discovers that he is of royal blood. For all Neal's American democratic sympathy he does not escape the romantic stereotyping of his hero—noble blood will tell even on the frontier. Through Harold's innocent eye, Neal effects some reputable satire of society; Harold is surprised at the expense lavished on public monuments when the funds could have been used to build a hospital. He visits the seat of rural charm, his ancestral home. He discovers the correspondence of Oscar and Elvira, and much of the volume reverts to epistolary style in recounting their love affair. Even more than Harold, Oscar has demonstrated the unleashed pride, will and ambition of a titan: "from head to foot, a creature of desperate energies, irregular appetite, and sublime incoherency . . ." (*L*, II, 124).

Suddenly Oscar returns from drowning, is reunited with Elvira, the woman he thought he had killed. Harold delivers an impassioned speech to parliament in defense of the nobility of the Indians, and they all depart for America. As they make a family pilgrimage to the spot of Logan's death, Fate appears as the maddened father of so many of the characters: Logan, not dead but totally mad. He shoots down Harold; Loena falls dead across his body. Oscar fights and kills Logan who dies "like some wild beast strangling in his own blood." Having killed his own father and having learned from Elvira of her shameful affairs, Oscar goes mad and dies. With most of the cast dead, this time without hope of surprise resurrection, Neal ends on a patriotic note, asking the English to "acknowledge us, as we are, the strongest (though boastful and arrogant) progeny of yourselves . . . when your nation was a collossus . . ." (*L*, II, 34).

The importance of *Logan* was in its demonstration of the uses of native material within the tradition of the gothic novel as developed by Charles Brockden Brown; in its foreshadowing of elements of the border romance, particularly the more bloody variety such as Robert Montgomery Bird's *Nick of the Woods* (1837); in its tracing of the effects of the sin of the father upon later members of the family—a theme that Hawthorne was to develop so brilliantly; in its elements of diseased psychology that Poe was soon to exploit. As both Cowie and Lease have amply shown, there are passages in Neal where dream— or rather nightmare—imagery is brilliantly used to reveal the trou-

bled soul of a character. Harold's near madness after learning of his
incestuous relations transforms the ship's ropes upon which he tries
to sleep into serpents of conscience:

Alas, for Harold! A continual and confused ringing was about him, all night
long. Worn, and trembling, and sick at heart, time appeared to stand still, as
he turned, again and again, and adjusted his limbs to the rugged cordage,
upon which he lay, until he was utterly exhausted. . . . And then his
conscience would awake, and put on her bloody robes, and sit over him with a
terrible countenance—and he would feel himself pinioned, naked, hand and
foot—helpless, alone—with just enough of light to see the far off and dim
movement of innumerable feet, incessantly approaching in the darkness, as
of some cumbrous, and interminable monster—and to feel ten thousand
detestable and obscene creatures crawling slowly over his very lips and eyes,
which he had no power to shut—slimy, loathsome reptiles, slipping lazily
over his naked fingers; while his very flesh crawled and quivered, and rotted,
in the poison that they left in their trail. Anon, this would be changed. The
light would break out upon him—he would be sleeping in a delicious green
solitude—the earth flowering all about him, with fountains flowing "in odour
and gold"—and violets—"but the trail of the serpent was over them all." (L,
I, 291).

As an experimental novel, the influence of the book was great upon
the rising generation of American writers, although it was not reprinted in America. To British readers it appealed on different
grounds as the work of an erratic but near genius of the New World.
Besides the 1822 edition, *Logan* was republished in London in 1840
and again in 1845. Today it is difficult to be fair to the book, for it is
excessive in almost every way. Perhaps the best evaluation is that of
Neal himself, writing from the perspective of England and seeing his
novel in the context of the then scant range of American fiction. In his
survey of American writers, he concludes,

Logan is full of power—eloquence—poetry—instinct, with a more than
mortal extravagance: Yet so crowded—so incoherent—. . . so outrageously
overdone, that no-body *can* read it through. Parts are without a parallel for
passionate beauty;—power of language: deep tenderness, poetry—yet every
page . . . is rank with corruption—the terrible corruption of genius.—It
should be taken, as people take opium. A grain may exhilarate—more may
stupify—much will be death.[21]

His next novel will be more controlled; he had passed through a personal crisis by projecting his own unresolved pride and ambition into his titans—Logan, Harold, and Oscar.

III   Seventy-Six

When he came to write *Seventy-Six* Neal found through the framework of history a greater control over his torrential prose, producing what he continued to feel was his best novel. Shortly after publication, pretending to be a British critic reviewing American literature, he treats his own work, and gives a fair summary of the achievement: "I pronounce this to be one of the best romances of the age. With a little care—some pruning: a few alterations, it might be made an admirable book of. So far as it goes, it is quite a faithful history of the old American War—told with astonishing vivacity. The reader becomes an eyewitness in spite of himself."[22] The seeming boast of the first sentence is a proper judgment, for *Seventy-Six* appeared in 1823, the same year as Cooper's *The Pioneers* and *The Pilot*. When he was writing it, virtually the only competition for Neal's new novel was Cooper's *The Spy* (1821) with which Neal's compares well in its evocation of actuality.

Neal had been in the preceding years filling himself to overflowing with reading for his share of Allen's *History of the American Revolution* (1819–1822). Now stimulated by Cooper's example, he drew on this historical background,[23] adding the zest of a style more personal and exciting than Cooper's. By narrating the story through the words of an old soldier, Jonathan Oadley, Neal gains the eyewitness viewpoint of a storyteller's story. Oadley ostensibly relates the events in the life of his brother, but they are events in which he also plays a part. From the moment of Oadley's opening words, "Yes, my children, I will no longer delay it," a colloquial tone of immediacy is set. Neal is deliberately experimenting with a new and American style of writing. Before him he had few models (and few after him until Twain) who tried to bring the prose of serious fiction closer to the speech of contemporary America. Earlier experiments had been restricted to stage Yankees like Jonathan of *The Contrast* or humorous newspaper pieces of frontier humor. Neal wanted to narrow the gap between spoken American English and the prevalent stilted style of romance. Even Natty Bumppo speaks in an elevated language for elevated thoughts, and as for the prose of *The Spy*, Neal found Cooper's style "without peculiarity—brilliancy, or force."[24] Neal's aim was to "talk on paper" (S, I, 17).

Oadley therefore begins to talk on paper, recording for his children an account of the family's participation in the Revolution. But first he warns them—and the reader—that the style will be unique:

My style may often offend you. I do not doubt that it will. I hope that it will. It will be remembered the better. It will be the style of a soldier, plain and direct, where facts are to be narrated; of a man, roused and inflamed, when the nature of man is outraged—of a father—a husband—a lover and a child, as the tale is of one, or of the other. (S, I, 17)

The very passage itself illustrates the directness of the soldier in the short sentences and repetition, but also the longer and looser sentence structure of passion—usually easily spotted on Neal's pages by the free use of dashes.[25]

Soon the language will reveal itself in another way as the language of soldiers; profanity and oaths occur with an outspokenness appropriate to the occasion, but nonethless surprising for the century. Especially from the fire-eating Clinton come frequent "damn its" and an occasional "what the devil." With complete vividness Clinton recounts the skirmish in which he was wounded:

"It was *there*," said he, "*there*, exactly where that horse is passing now, that they first fired upon me. I set off at speed up that hill, but, finding nine of the party there, I determined to dash over that elevation in front—I attempted it, but, shot after shot, was fired after me, until I preferred making one desperate attempt, sword in hand, to being shot down, like a fat goose, upon a broken gallop. I wheeled, made a dead set, at the son-of-a-bitch in my rear, unhorsed him, and actually broke through the line." (S, I, 184–85)

Not until a century later was the same freedom allowed a writer; even the Twain of *Roughing It* reports a profane miner's oath as a "son of a skunk." Neal's frankness, of course, did not slip unrebuked past the critics, who faulted him for attributing oaths to the speech of honorable soldiers.[26]

In the dialogues, obviously, Neal is most able to achieve the effects of "talking on paper." He is bothered by the conventional labelling of speeches, and struggles to gain some variety through direct address (S, I, 131), then midway in the novel, he tries another device: the narrator speaks for him: "To save the constant repetition of *said he*, and *said she*—I shall give the names first, of each speaker, as in a dialogue [That is, as in a play]" (S, I, 198). He tries this for a time, but soon slips back to more traditional means of identifying speakers.

This, however, was only the first of Neal's attempts to make his dialogue more closely approximate the look as well as the sound of actual talk. In later novels he continued experimentation and actually found a more adequate solution.

This pursuit of a more colloquial style also had a salutary effect on Neal's narrative and descriptive passages. The images of meteors and cataracts that overweight his early poetry and prose—especially in *Logan*—are replaced from closer to earth. As a result Neal's writing at this period contains some of his most telling comparisons. For instance, he describes how the soldiers only become aware of their discomforture after the heat of battle cools: ". . . and then it was—*then*—when it was necessary to move about the quieter operations of strife, that we began to feel the intense coldness of the night—the keen air cutting into our new wounds, like rough broken glass" (*S*, II, 160). The cutting of the winter air is realized with a vividness that can only make the feelings of the troops come alive on the readers' senses. Neal draws on natural observation to find a simile for the pent-up fury—and evil—of Copely: ". . . he opened his mouth, and his heart ran out, like a current dammed up,—and ready, at his bidding, to waste and thunder, like the spring tide, and swollen rivers of our country, loaded with ice, and foam, and blackened with wreck and ruin" (*S*, II, 79). When the same demonic Copely turns his enmity toward the narrator, the effect is more than chilling: ". . . my heart, upon my word, felt, as if it had been drifting about in a cold rain, for a week, drenched and soaked through—chilled" (*S*, II, 76). There is, of course, a certain heightened straining after special effect in such passages. But the style is capable of quiet understatement as well. A family interlude ends with the men departing once again for the battlefield. "Rodman and Copely then embraced their wives . . . and . . . set off, at full speed, from the house. It was a bitter cold morning for the season" (*S*, II, 222). The restraint of the final sentence, which is also the last sentence of the paragraph and chapter, is more powerful than all of Neal's earlier pyrotechnics in *Logan*.

Furthermore, the plot is the most straightforward that Neal has so far developed. While dramatizing the darkest days of the Revolution through the battles of New Jersey and on to Valley Forge, he also traces the adventures of the Oadley family—two brothers, a cousin, father, and friends. As the story opens the family has not yet been touched by the war and they debate whether the young men should enter service. When the Hessians burn their home and rape their mother, there is a rush to enlist. The young men mature and marry during their years of service. Archibald, the Byronic brother of the narrator and hero of the novel, has to kill two men in duels, but is afterward haunted by the blood he has spilled. Historical personages including Washington, Lafayette, Pulaski, and Burr appear briefly. The events of war are intertwined with the romances of the young men. The central couple, Archibald and Lucia, are ill-fated as each is tainted by sins of passion; the novel ends with their marriage at which Archibald falls dead. The scene and line end the novel in Neal's best (or worst) melodramatic manner. Archibald murmurs "Lucia, my *wife*" and then

He stood suddenly erect upon his feet; the light flashed over his face. It was the face of a dead man. He fell upon the floor: a loud shriek followed. Where were we?—*Where*! We ran to him—we raised him up. It was too late! Almighty God! *it was too late!* HIS WIFE WAS A WIDOW! (*S*, II, 260)

It is not for such overwrought effects that the novel still appeals, but rather for the actualization of battle scenes from the viewpoint of ordinary soldiers, for honestly presented love affairs of real young men and women, for some touches of social comedy, and for the use of psychological material of visions and dreams.

One of the most effective battle scenes presents the retreat across the icy river at Trenton. When one of the great war chargers falls into the river and is carried downstream and under the ice, Jonathan recalls that " . . . either of us would have risked his own life, I have no doubt, for the safety of the animal—when we heard his last loud, convulsive sobbing, and saw the amazing strength of his blows, as he broke through the ice at every leap" (*S*, I, 165). Here as elsewhere, Neal is particularly good in dealing with horses; one of the best sections of his poem "The Battle of Niagara" had presented the night movements of the cavalry, and the passages in *Seventy-Six* dealing with cavalry remain stirring today.

Well presented is the enmity and rivalry between the Northern and Southern troops fighting under Washington. While Neal's native sympathy goes to the New Englanders as the "most substantial men for the service" (*S*, II, 39), he is fair in his praise for the more chivalric valor of the Virginians.

Interspersed with the historical scenes of battle is a secondary plot of romance. At a time when the daughters of Pamela dominated fiction, Neal's women, in contrast, are varied, warm, and even earthy. His lovers act as real young men and women involved in real affairs of the heart in which sexual attraction is felt on both sides. Archibald's love for Lucia falters when the seducer Copely comes between them for a time, but even in the role of seducer he is far from the stock villain of the sentimental novel. He is a brave officer, a close relative to Washington, who is admired for his good qualities by Archibald who is deeply affected by the developing triangle. The reader feels the impending tragedy of a situation that can only end in a challenge and duel. Archibald wins but suffers remorse that undermines both health and mind.

Concurrently Archibald's brother, the narrator Jonathan, is in love with Lucia's haughty sister Clara, but cannot resist the vivacity of flirtatious blonde Ellen. On leave in Philadelphia he finds himself alone with Ellen; the scene develops warmly, stopping just short of physical seduction, although it is a good question who seduces whom. Only Jonathan's sense of honor controls the situation. After the first passionate kiss upon the mouth, Jonathan remembers Clara and breaks off the love scene with the suggestion that they cool off with a walk through the snowy streets of the city. He admonishes Ellen that her flirtatious ways would with anyone else have been her undoing; he had only been teaching her a needed lesson! In this pious conclusion, Neal is himself involved. As a young bachelor, he had been caught out and "misunderstood" in a similar situation with the sister-in-law of his friend Pierpont.[27]

With Ellen, Neal is presenting the realities of passion among the young and their complications. Jonathan still has to face Clara who has heard an exaggerated report of his behavior with Ellen. After she is convinced of his innocence, the scene develops into a love exchange which Neal breaks off, this time less effectively, by a Shandean device: At the crucial moment, the page is filled with asterisks and a note from the publisher to the effect that a whole page has been lost. The story takes up again as the lovers are parting (S, II, 111).

The love plots take place in the private homes of New Jersey and Philadelphia, allowing both for good insights into the effects of the Revolution upon domestic life and for scenes of social comedy. There are, for example, playful hits against the social awkwardness of some Quaker men: " . . . haw! haw! haw!—laughed the brace of Quakers, sprawling their legs about, and, leaning back in their chairs, with their hands in their breeches" (S, II, 241). At the opposite extreme are the overly ladylike airs of Lucia's and Clara's mother. Married to the Frenchman M. Arnauld, she likes to embellish her conversation with mangled French and Italian, an innocent ridiculousness which

Neal satirizes (for example, S, I, 199–200). Neal's love of punning, however, gets out of hand when the discussion turns to the dog of Venice, the dolphin of France, and the clam of Tartary (S, I, 242). He is on surer ground with Yankee humor. A Down-East frontiersman named Hanson is serving in the army and brings news of Archibald. Ill at ease in the drawing room, Hanson shifts about in his chair, crosses his legs, tugs at the collar of his coat, and then reports in good Yankee dialect. The entire passage, of several pages, possesses a linguistic interest. Hanson gradually loses his shyness as he recounts the battle in which Archibald was wounded, and his terse, broken speech rises to Yankee rhetoric as he concludes: "Captain Rodman too, did famously; but the major!—well—Guns! how he rattled away at 'em!—hey—no quarter—none!—It soon became a race—whoop! Morgan's riflemen peppered 'em, fore and aft, well—the horse tumbled together, in heaps. . . . So, you see, they got a sound drubbin' " (S, II, 203). As elsewhere, Neal uses the dash freely to indicate the pauses and rhythms of actual speech. The passage also reveals the New England use of "famously" in the sense of "well." The archaic plural "horse" is true to the dialect as is the use of words like "drubbin' " and "peppered."

Some of the same broken rhythms of speech are found in remarkable passages of dream psychology used by Neal to reveal the inner passions of his characters. In a state that would be recognized today as battle fatigue, Jonathan's sleep is troubled with war images:

I was asleep. At dead of midnight, I heard a trumpet, as I thought, sounding to battle. I rose, pained and dizzy,—unwilling to go out—and desirous to skulk, if I could, into the holes of the rocks. Then I thought that it began to rain fire upon me; and the earth shook, and battalions of men, armed all over in shining mail, spattered with blood, came, parading, column after column, from the earth—nation after nation—each of loftier, and yet loftier stature still,—warlike—and terrible, like the buried Apostles of liberty: and then, all at once, there was a tremendous explosion, and I felt myself sinking in a swamp—the loose earth quivering like jelly, at every tread, and cold serpents and bloated toads all slipping about me, so thickly, that, set my naked foot, wherever I would, something that had life in it—some fat icy reptile would stir under the pressure—and then I was entangled in the thorny creeping tendrils of many a plant that encumbered my path; dead bodies lay in my way; I was pinioned hand and foot, and serpents fed upon my blood, and vultures flapped over me. And then, out of the east, there blazed, all at once, a light, like a million of rockets, that blinded me. And then, I felt a hand—the hand of a murderer about my throat—God! (S, II, 54–5)

Similar use of psychological material reveals the approaching breakup of Archibald and the reactions of Jonathan to battle itself. Unlike his brother, Jonathan was not eager to enlist and confesses his fear of battle. As he reports his first battle, however, he reveals the excitement and "terrible delight" that catches him up until he fights with "a sort of religious fervour, exceeding wrath and indignation." He is knocked from his horse, senseless; when he comes to, the battlefield is dark and strewn with corpses. He staggers toward an enemy soldier, but the heat of battle is gone and he feels no hatred but sympathy for a fellow human being. Not until the scenes of *The Red Badge of Courage* were the varying emotions of war to be so well realized—and, interestingly, both Neal and Crane were of the generation after the war which each vivifies. An act of creative imagination brings both battle and soldier's reaction to life, as Robert Bain has correctly stated regarding this battle scene: "Neal explores in some depth, the consciousness of his narrator. The fear, the chaos, the exhilaration, the righteousness, the madness, the emptiness, the amazement, and finally the exhaustion are realized fictionally in the world outside Oadley *and* in his consciousness. . . ."[28] This realization is largely effected by repetition of highly sensuous imagery and contrasts of light and dark, noise and quiet, hatred and sympathy.

To dramatize thus the inner and outer battles has taken greater space than Neal had planned for. The reader is therefore not surprised by Oadley's sudden cry "I shall never be able to carry you through the whole war, as I intended to do, when I began" (*S*, II, 242). In the few remaining pages of the novel, the events are summarized by the use of letters that culminate in the final dramatized scene of Archibald's marriage and death. Nor is that last scene the only touch of gothicism in the story. Archibald has visions, a mysterious rapping three times is heard just before the death of the father, violent storms in the elements accompany storms of the passions in a deliberate reaching after an effect of the sublime. In fact, the sublimity of American nature is explicitly discussed by Archibald:

Let a man go with me . . . out into the wilderness . . . sit with me as we sat together this afternoon, before the hurricane broke down upon us; and feel the soft air whispering about his heart; or hear the thunder breaking at his feet; and see the great trees bending and parting, in the wind and blackness of God's power—I care not who he is, or what he is—where born—or how educated—I defy him not to fall down, with his forehead in the dust, and acknowledge the presence of God. (*S*, II, 234)

It was not this reverential effect of the sublime, however, that infused Neal's next novels. In these he returned to the more extravagant style of *Logan* in order to explore human passion.

CHAPTER 3

The Novel of Justification

A S offshoots of his superheated writing of *Logan*, Neal had in 1822
written the greater part of two other novels, but laid them aside
to respond to Cooper's *The Spy* with *Seventy-Six*. He then returned
to the drafts, augmenting them with opinion and self-justification
before publishing them in 1823. He failed of London publication,
however, for the digressions—original though they were felt to
be—were judged of insufficient interest to the general reader of
novels.[1]

I Randolph

With *Randolph* and *Errata* Neal was once again experimenting
with the form of the novel, developing it as a vehicle of opinion.
Perhaps influenced by Fielding, he included essays on a range of
topics: history, education, public welfare, art, literature. On his own
he included large doses of self-justification. As a result, the plot of
Randolph fades into the background, overshadowed by the digressions which comprise two-thirds of the book. However, given Neal's
penchant for gothic obscurities of plot, the loss is largely gain: the
modern reader is more interested in his flashing insights and strong
opinions than in dark doings of superheroes and heroines.

The opinions are often memorable; for example, he characterizes a
host of literary figures with a telling sentence or two: (John Milton) "A
great man—but much learning hath made him mad"; "He was of the
ancient school, who wrestled, and ate, and slept in their heavy
armour . . ."; (Thomas Moore) "never great"; "a well-trained singing
bird"; (Henry Milman) "metallick brilliancy"; "Leaf-gold is not thin
enough for him" (*R*, II, 36); (William Wordsworth) "a great, plain-
hearted, august simpleton" "a giant blind in both eyes" (*R*, II, 32–33);
(Robert Southey) [his power is to make] "great poetry, appear
commonplace; and commonplace poetry, great" (*R*, II, 33).

The thrusts are brilliant, as are his comments on a host of American writers including Percival, Everett, Pierpont, Dana, C. B. Brown, Irving, Paulding, Cooper, Paul Allen (*R*, I, 135–139, 141–143; II, 209–210). Including himself in the discussions, he deliberately misspells his name as Neale, an author whose style he declares is "overflowing with start and turbulence . . . which he thinks fine writing." He adds advice he could seldom take: "Let him learn a little discretion—subdue his hot temper—hurry less, in his manifestation of feeling . . ." (*R*, I, 139–141).

Also included is some of the very first criticism of American artists: Gilbert Stuart, John Trumbull, Benjamin West, Thomas Sully, Samuel Morse, Washington Allston, the Peale family, John Vanderlyn (*R*, II, 107–38). Likewise, Neal's first drama criticism also appears, discussing Thomas Cooper, James Wallack, Sarah Siddons, Edmund Kean. This material as well as that dealing with American writers was to be expanded for his series in *Blackwood's* a few years later. For the social historian there are vignettes of American towns, including a number that Neal knew well. His hero and heroine travel from the South into Maine, and beyond to Quebec, reporting on Portsmouth, Saco, Kennebunk, Portland (" . . . one of the most delightful places . . . to be found in the world. The weather is charming . . . [*R*, I, 322]). In part these descriptions of American towns were aimed at correcting errors Neal found in Jedediah Morse's famous school geography.

Such essaylike digressions came easily to a novel written in the outmoded epistolary style. The main plot concerns the Byronic Edward Molton and the efforts of lovely Sarah Ramsay to determine whether or not he is the seducer and murderer he is reputed to be. A subplot deals with the affairs of Juliet and the conspiracy to marry her off unworthily to clear the field for her companion Ann. Molton's letters to a British correspondent, in dealing with a host of American topics, serve to reveal his genius. The action moves northward until, in Maine, Sarah finds herself followed by a terrifying deaf and dumb man, and then protected by a kindly Spencer Randolph (the titular hero). Both, it turns out, are in reality the titanic Edward Molton.

Discussions of literature by Molton gave Neal a chance to develop further his own aesthetic,[3] while discussion of American writers led him to explore the state of the arts in the New World, concluding that

. . . we have no "dramatists"—no "architects"—no "sculptors"—no "musicians"—no "tragedians." And why? It is not for want of natural genius.

There is enough of that among my countrymen. It is for the want of encouragement, riches, a crowded population, luxury, and corruption. These arts are the last, to which a people turn their attention. (*R*, II, 202)

But like most of his contemporaries[4] he foresees a better day coming:

The time is rapidly approaching, when, it will be enough to sell a work, if it be called American. We are getting to feel a national pride; and men are already beginning to put in their title pages, *"by an American"*—and *"an American tale"*—words, that, a few years ago, would have been as politick as "by a Choctaw. . . ." (*R*, II, 209)

But the novel itself was less a blow struck for American literature than a riposte by Neal against enemies, real or imagined.

The excessive and bristling defence of honor that so characterizes his fictional heroes—Archibald, Molton, Will Adams—was a central part of his own make-up. For instance, the struggling young lawyer is needlessly harsh on revered members of the Baltimore bar. He includes hits at Attorney General Wirt (*R*, II, 234–35) after having referred to him with low humor as "a Wirt or Wart" (*R*, II, 156). His fullest attack was reserved, however, for William Pinckney, a well-thought-of and prominent lawyer. Neal finds in him no real eloquence, but only sound and fury, suggesting that one could tell the size of his fee by the quantity of sound he emitted in court (*R*, II, 156, 235). Although he admitted that Pinckney was the "greatest lawyer of America," he found him "no gentleman," a vulgar fellow compounded of "part English Bully and part English Dandy" (*R*, II, 235–36). (Pinckney had served on a diplomatic mission in Britain, returning to Baltimore in 1811.) The attack might have gone unnoticed had Pinckney not died while the novel was at the printers. Instead of suppressing his attack, Neal added a footnote that made matters worse; in it he explains that death changes nothing; there will be no retraction, for truth must be honored.

But Neal had not counted on another Byronic poet and hot-head besides himself; such, however, was the son Edward Coote Pinckney, who had just returned to Baltimore. He promptly challenged Neal to a duel. As the author of *Keep Cool* and its attack on the *code duello*, Neal was in no position to comply. He refused and was posted as a coward. This was in the fall of 1823 when Neal was seeing *Errata* through the press; he was just in time to add a self-exculpating postscript as his answer to Pinckney. Neal reprints the letters of young Pinckney and himself, includes a copy of the handbill posting him as a coward, and retreats not a whit from his prior position. In fact, he adds the details of the father's habit of picking his nose in public and of wiping his nose on his cuff. To the title page, he adds, "By a coward."

If Neal did not acquit himself well in the Pinckney affair, he was consistent to his professions against duelling. The Yankee in all his stubbornness had met in Edward Coote Pinckney the very "caricature of the duelling young Southerner."[5]

Other personal attacks are more or less obscured by the use of initials or nicknames (Joe for the Joseph Lord of Neal's business venture). A number of private feuds in *Randolph* are now probably beyond recovery, although Richards speculates about them. He is probably correct that Mr. P——is John Pierpont and the Mr. S——, who slighted Neal, is Jared Sparks.[6] He is certainly correct in identifying an episode in Neal's bachelor life; Lease, following Richards,[7] unravels most of the episode and shows how it led to a cooling of the Neal-Pierpont friendship. Both Richards and Lease are right in seeing a biographical source for Neal's repeated fictional scene of near-seduction, and they struggle to unravel fact from fiction. It is not necessary, however, at this date to try to clear or darken Neal's reputation as an interrupted seducer[8] (Richards says it cannot be done, anyway). Rather, it is more profitable to ask what literary use Neal as author makes of a personal event of strong psychological impact. An exploration of this psychological source of Neal's fiction will follow a discussion of the novel that appeared within a month of *Randolph* and is a companion piece. *Errata* was to be the concluding novel in Neal's early series of fiction, for in late December, 1823, he would be on ship for England and a magazine career.

II   Errata

From the perspective of England, Neal reviewed somewhat objectively his writing of the Baltimore years. Choosing to overlook his initial effort *Keep Cool* (1817), he saw a pattern to the four remaining novels written in the intense period of 1822–1823. In the pages of *Blackwood's* he declares that "LOGAN is a piece of *declamation;* SEVENTY-SIX, of *narrative;* RANDOLPH, *epistolary;* ERRATA, or WILL ADAMS, *colloquial*—They are a complete series; a course of experiment. . . ."[9] While there is truth in the descriptive word Neal applies to each novel, and while it is true that each novel is experimental, his retrospective view saw more overall purpose than existed at the time of composition.

In truth *Errata* is the fullest development to date of Neal's use of colloquialism for fiction. The preface directly states his intent: "I have written this tale, for the purpose of showing how people talk, when they are not talking for display; when they are telling a story of themselves, familiarly; seated about their own firesides; with plenty of apples and cider; in the depth of winter. . . ."[10] The result is some of the best "talking on paper" that Neal produced, but just as unfortunately, his colloquialism is combined with rambling. He now terms his new style "natural writing" which he defines as "what *anybody,* in the same situation, would naturally *say—if he could . . .* broken and incoherent, at times—for such is the language of passion . . ." (*E,* I, 59). For a writer seeking after natural language, the models of Addison's "simpering, smooth, sweet, musical cadence" and Johnson's "great, lumbering, heavy, windy, pompous, lubberly movement" are downright detrimental. Instead the writer should observe the difference between a man talking and the same man orating; natural writing will follow the model of actual talk (*E,* II, 13–14).

In setting forth the talk of his hero Will Adams, Neal, however, lets him ramble until both style and organization collapse into formlessness. The result is a ranting fictional life of the narrator, Will Adams, and of the hunchback Hammond, both of whom are projections of Neal in his varied activities and propensities—unhappy childhood, egotism, energy, forthright honesty, capacity for work. Also contributing to the formlessness is the influence of Sterne. The Shandyism that had lent a strange ambivalence of tone to Neal's first novel resurfaces in *Errata.* Mock footnotes pretend that the editor has made some devastating attack on the text, by commenting "This is stolen from Byron," or noting for a humorous passage, "Joe Miller, 1st ed., p. 13, & 14." Chapter 7 of the first volume provides another example. The entire chapter is one page in length and discusses the use of asterisks to gain an effect of the risqué, ending: "What have I said? Nothing. I have only stopped—thrown down my eyes—and minced my words, a little—as modest ladies do—when— * * * * etc." Neal had, of course, used just this device himself in a racey love scene in *Seventy-Six.*

Like *Randolph,* the loose form of *Errata* also allows Neal to include essays on a variety of topics: he attacks the nonlanguage of Quakers, argues for correct pronunciation ("Nothing is trivial that has a right and a wrong"); takes exception to a decision of Chief Justice Marshall; argues for a national bank for issuance of currency; and acts as an expert on the rearing of children (As a father, years later, even Neal was less sure of this thorny subject).

Even in the novel Neal could not resist the role of teacher. Born into a family of educators—father, mother, twin sister—he had the teacher's natural inclination to share his own learning with others. His later school of gymnastics and his public lectures arose from the same sources as these mini-essays within the novels. Self-educated himself, he offered the means of intellectual improvement to others.

He has much to say on education generally, and his remarks take good account of child psychology of the Hartley school; he urges inculcating good principles from infancy onward by associating pain with wrong and pleasure with right. Further, adults must always carry out whatever is promised a child in order to establish the sacredness of the word once given and of truth-telling. From his own unhappy experience, he urges parents and teachers to treat the child as an adult as soon as possible (E, II, 279–95).

It was outrage done to his budding manhood that caused Neal to carry into adulthood bitter resentment against his own schoolmaster Stephen Patten. Continuing the self-justification of *Randolph*, he now paid off an old debt by pillorying Patten through the reminiscences of Adams. Speaking of his school teachers, Adams proclaims "Among the first . . . was a precious jack-ass, named STEPHEN PATTEN, a school-master, to whom it was my misfortune to be sent . . ." (E, I, 59). He goes on to picture Patten as a tyrant of the town (that is, charity) school.

Indeed, Patten, who had arrived in Portland the year of Neal's birth, had a reputation as a stern disciplinarian who had even turned his ferule on an assistant who had dared to question him on the matter of punishment.[11] Years later, Neal is still smarting from an unjust whipping. He has Adams tell of bringing a note excusing his absence. "But MASTER PATTEN was not to be trifled with. He first flogged me, and then read the billet. . . . For this, I never forgave him" (E, I, 62). Neal's revenge was both intemperate and ill-advised. The Portland to which Neal returned in 1827 respected the aging Patten (he died in 1855, just under ninety years of age), and the town greeted its famous author—for this and other indiscretions—with utter hostility. Like many another author of autobiographical bent, Neal found it difficult to go home again when he had printed too many unvarnished truths.[12] He had not foreseen that the citizens "would care a snap for the stories I told, whether true or false . . ." (*WR*, 328). Neal had also outraged the now powerful Willis family by Hammond's recounting the tricks of the trade of an apprentice shopkeeper—again Neal himself very thinly disguised (*E*, I, 65–67).

Other autobiographical details concerning the retail business in Baltimore (*E*, II, 90–92), supporting himself by his writing (*E*, II, 107–108), and his expulsion by the Quakers (*E*, I, 257) were only less inflammatory.

This was a mistaken use of his own experiences. He was right in assuming that storytelling is fiction in which "memory is pieced out with imagination,"[13] but no imagination added to or transmuted the attack on Master Patten. With Patten he made sure by printing the name in full, in capital letters. Neal's memories were put to better literary use in description of social events: a barn raising, a husking bee, bundling (*E*, II, 50–51), and a revival campmeeting (*E*, I, 274–76). At the last of these, his narrator decides to try a little "conversion" of his own on a pretty girl, is caught, and asked by the elders to leave. The episode is one of many related by Adams, who has the same ungentlemanly quality of telling after kissing as Molton in *Randolph*.

In a long passage, Adams fancies himself in love and surveys all the possible girls who might be the object, rejecting each in turn. In his portrait of the brash country girl who makes all the advances, there is excellent humor as well as some sly touches for the prurient. One of those satirized is an Eliza S (possibly an old flame of Neal's), a girl "so touched with theatrical romance, that, to carry her heart . . . it is only necessary to make love, like a man on horseback . . ." (*E*, I, 263–65).

Neal's fictional women usually show a susceptibility to passion. Refreshingly direct in an age of sentimentality is his modern-sounding attribution to woman of "a constantly operating attraction toward man, which God meant to be *irresistible*—or nearly so. . . . You [women] have passions like men—stronger indeed; or you are dealt partially with. . ." (*E*, II, 247). While he grants women their sexuality, he also inveighs against what he considers flagrant feminine behavior. Marrying for money is no better than whoring (*E*, I, 132). Following fashion and thus appearing publicly in low-cut gowns is immodest:

. . . you go with your very bosoms naked, aye, your *bosoms*, whereon, if a man really loved you, he would as soon another had placed his hand, or his mouth, as his eyes; aye, your *bosoms*—the pillow, where a husband . . . will yet lay his aching temples, with the thought of rapture—that he sleeps upon something holy—unvisited, unprofaned. (*E*, I, 136)

In the cause of morality, Neal is here swept beyond the line of good taste, yet the vehemence and outspokenness is healthier than the Victorian repression that was fast descending. It is refreshing to find Neal arguing against the new fastidiousness that would avoid speaking of a pain in the breast or leg or thigh. With justice he finds that euphemisms often inflame the imagination and reveal a real immodesty on the part of the person using them (*E*, I, 131).

Women or, more precisely, the sexual passion for women is an underlying cause of the violence in *Will Adams*. It is unreasoning sexual jealousy that causes him to suspect Hammond and his wife of infidelity; he challenges the innocent Hammond, who, refusing to fight, is shot down. Adams is ultimately driven mad by the knowledge of Hammond's innocence and his wife's tragic death, but not before he has also shown insane jealousy toward his sister Elizabeth. He had assumed with a crypto-incestuous love that Elizabeth's vow never to marry arose from her love for him; when he discovers that Hammond is the cause—"not her love to *me* "—his jealousy breaks forth anew (*E*, II, 260). Such passion might be only the usual stuff of melodrama, except that Neal is interested in the roots of emotion. The long reminiscing passages about Adams' childhood are an exploration into the psychological sources of his later troubles. Spoiled by his mother before her death, he is terrified of his brutal father and is soon cast adrift to make his own way in the world. As David Davis has noted,[14] Neal is applying a version of the Oedipus myth to explain the impulsive duellist: the flashing desire to kill rides on childhood passions of fear and jealousy.

Herein lies the reason for Neal's use of his own life story in *Errata*. The temper of Adams is much like that of Neal himself. While Neal had lost a father to Adams' mother, the story of their boyhoods is otherwise close.[15] Even the figure of Hammond arises from a dwarf George who worked in one of the bookstores of Portland during Neal's growing years. As a poor but proud Quaker boy, dressed in outmoded Quaker fashion, Neal was subjected to cruel taunts and physical harm by the roughnecks of Portland until he overcame his Quaker teaching and learned to fight back. But out of the deeply felt injuries he developed an overkeen sense of honor and was ever quick to strike out at a real or fancied affront. Necessary as it was to him, he yet feared his own temper. He was haunted by a childhood accident when he had struck and injured a comrade. The fear that he might have committed murder remained with him through life, vitalizing the varying scenes of his haunted duellists from Archibald through Adams. In terms of his fiction, this early episode with its near tragic results of violence was one of two experiences that were central traumas of his life. (The other event—even more important to Neal's character and thence to his fiction—was his youthful visit to the bedroom of a fourteen-year-old girl.)

Fear of his own violence played a large role in Neal's image of himself. His autobiography delves into his childhood for sources similar to those of Will Adams. One whole chapter entitled "Quarrel-some or Not?" explores his childhood fisticuffs, his being disowned by the Quakers, and his sparring overseas. Anecdotes about Neal by contemporaries often illustrate his quick temper; when over seventy he threw an insulting man off the trolley car as on an earlier occasion he threw an offending Irishman down the stairs from his law office (WR, 87). Of his temper itself, one observer wrote:

> Mr. Neal is quick as a flash. Get him angry, and woe to your devoted head. The color leaves his face and a cataract of words falls from his lips, while you are in fear of instant annihilation. . . . But Neal's temper is soon over. Call upon him half an hour after a torrent of invective, and ten to one he will take you by the hand, and beg a thousand pardons for his rashness. . . .[16]

What emerges from the portrait is a basically sensitive and kindly man whose pride was like a raw nerve. At the least touch, the response was massive, even frightening. In part his temperament was a result of the genteel poverty in which a proud and brilliant boy grew up, grew into a brilliant but erratic man with many acquaintances but few friends—really only one, John Pierpont. He was thus often misunderstood as he engaged in public broils. He would fight and attack, for his world was a lonely one in which he made his way, neither expecting nor getting aid. In fact, the one thing he was unable to stand was a kindness.[17] He expected kindness only from the very few who penetrated his carefully built public defenses—his mother, his sister, his friend. From these he demanded no less than total acceptance of himself, a demand that Pierpont failed to meet in the Abby Lord situation.

In short, Neal was himself much like his fictional titans—Archibald, Molton, Will Adams. A mode of behavior may have been found in the literary type popularized by C. B. Brown, Godwin, and

Byron; but the basic lineaments of characters were projections of the author himself. The same Byronic protagonists also provided a means of Neal's coming to grips with his sexual trauma—an embarrassing episode with Pierpont's sister-in-law, Abby Lord.

III   *Personal Trauma—Fictional Justification*

To understand the central trauma of Neal's experience with Abby Lord, one must approach through his passionate nature. A bachelor until his mid-thirties, he had perhaps more than his share of romantic affairs. From these a certain amount of sexual guilt struggled against his New England conscience and his Quaker-born honesty. In fact, honesty with Neal was almost pathological in its compulsion to tell all. Truth at any cost was with him a way of life. In the area of sex, this need to speak out was ambiguously compounded partly of bragging and partly of confessing. His friend John Pierpont was cast in the roles of male confidant for the braggart and father confessor for the outcast Quaker. Between the years of twenty-seven and thirty, Neal's correspondence with Pierpont recounts all too often the sexual scrapes. For example, in 1820 he is writing a letter to pass the time until the arrival of his mistress; the titillating situation ends without the girl's arrival: "She hasn't come. The hour is past. And I am—all resignation! having made about as good use of this sheet of paper as I would of her, in getting rid of my lasciviousness" (March 4, 1820)[18] One role for the friend is to be an outlet for a lusty young man's sensual thoughts. Pierpont responds with wit as well as admonishment to a variety of amusing episodes such as an "elopement" with a Dutch girl that ends in Neal's undignified escape out a second story window just ahead of an irate father's bullet.[19]

In 1821 he is involved with Rosalba, daughter of Rembrandt Peale. Like Neal's favorite heroines (Clara, for example, in *Seventy-Six*), she unites "loftiness and innocence," but the romance is ended when "she found me out, and sent me adrift." Neal is still on good terms, however, with the artist's family two years later when he sits for two portraits.[20]

In the meantime Neal has befriended a beautiful and young Mrs. Howard who becomes his mistress. To Pierpont he justifies the relationship as built on the hope of "saving a fellow creature." Besides, the physical acts were only a "species of intemperence like occasional drinking."[21] Apparently in an attempt to break off, he sends her to Boston to launch a stage career, suggesting that his friend not only help her but share her—"let there be a *piece* between my *seed* and thy *seed*," he lewdly and impiously suggests (November 13, 1820).

None of this sexual bantering troubles the close relationship of the two men. Pierpont—like Twain's Reverend Joseph Twitchell— probably enjoyed the spice of his more rollicking correspondent. But when the escapades touched his family circle, toleration strains and breaks. What was eventually to estrange the two men started in 1818 and continued to 1823.

At the time of his trip back to visit his mother in Maine, Neal stopped over in Boston, boarding with Pierpont's brother-in-law Joseph (Joe) Lord. The three men had been former business partners. Also living with Joe was a fourteen-year-old sister Abby. Neal's and her bedrooms were next to each other. One night Neal stole into Abby's room and bed; she awoke, cried out ("how she squalled," wrote Neal), and Neal fled before the family arrived. There the matter might have ended, but self-justifying truth must be told. Neal feels impelled to write Pierpont to explain that he had been sleep-walking. Joe had been seen kissing an old flame of Neal's; jealousy like that of Will Adams made it impossible for Neal to forgive or forget. His emotions aswirl, he fell asleep that fatal night to dream that the newly married Joe asked him to test the wife's faithfulness. He dreamed of being led to her bed, of jumping in, and at a cry awakening to find himself with Abby. Unbelievable as the explanation was, Pierpont counseled letting the matter drop, reporting that Abby, possibly suspecting the truth, was half-convinced she had been dreaming.

But Neal cannot let it or Abby alone; he is back in Boston the following year. The family has in the meanwhile arranged for the precocious Abby an engagement, which Neal's presence and possible indiscretions endanger. The family closes ranks against Neal, and Pierpont opts to support the family position. The sensitive Neal demands full support and confidence from any friend; he will never feel the same about Pierpont again; he writes in terms appropriate to the fiction of the day: "You have shown me that it is foolish . . . to *confess* that one has been a scoundrel; but that, if a man must be a scoundrel—or *villain*—it is better to hold his tongue. He that is honest *beyond other men* . . . in telling his own shame—will, one day or other learn, as I have, that he had better be *more* of a villain—and hold his tongue . . ." (July 7, 1823).

His justification now moves to his fiction where in *Randolph* the Abby incident is thinly disguised. This time he offers a different explanation. His alter ego Molton had only been teaching an innocent but foolish girl a lesson. Perhaps Neal came to believe in this final version, for in its essential outline it was the justification of all his titans of the period. In *Logan* there is Harold's ambiguous rape of Elvira. In *Seventy-Six* Jonathan is virtually engaged to Sarah—but cannot resist the lively Ellen, controlling himself only to teach the young flirt the dangers of her behavior. There is a repetition with Molton and Sarah of *Randolph* until in *Errata* he makes the factual basis all too abundantly clear. In the latter novel Will relates the warmest version of the scene yet. As a boarder, he is visited in his room by Caroline, a young girl of the family. Under emotional stress, she faints, her bosom is exposed, he loses control and plants his "passionate mouth to her bosom"—but steps are heard. The parents misunderstand and do not believe the innocence of the couple (*E*, I, 286–325). Then in a postscript, Neal defends the novel's "private history" as the last recourse of a man when he is not believed; he has written a book to refute "vile and wicked calumny" (*E*, II, 345–46).

By this time, repeated rendering public of his private history has perfected Neal's story. His autobiographical heroes are no seducer-villains, but men of moral strength. Under the enormous temptation of having a young girl—weakly betrayed by her own emotions as well as by inexperience—totally in his power, the superman controls himself in order to teach a needed lesson to a budding flirt—an early American Lolita. He is revealed to be no European seducer but an honest—although misunderstood—American Christian gentleman. For as Rosenberg brilliantly demonstrates, a middle-class sexual ideal was developing in nineteenth-century America, whereby "The Christian gentleman was an athlete of continence, not coitus, continuously testing his manliness in the fire of self-denial."[22] By triumphing over feelings, the gentleman developed a self-control that allowed the higher emotions of love to emerge—spiritual affinities.[23]

Neal's fictional self-justification will be the mode of the next decades of American ideal behavior. Like Falstaff defending his cowardice from instinct, Neal will be able to think the better of himself for the Abby episode. As a truly moral superman he had sought the inflaming occasion only to test his strength of will, enjoying his power over the helpless girl, and attaining a superiority over her by his self-control as a Christian and gentleman. In this way the romantic superman of German and Byronic romanticism was tamed to the moral climate of New England, and for Neal a self-acceptance of his conflicting passionate and moral natures is made possible. He had been born into the last of the eighteenth century when the lustier male prerogatives over the female (Tom Jones in the bushes with Molly) were giving way to the coming sentiment of a new morality. In the early 1820s Neal is caught between the two worlds at a time of emotional crisis in his own life. The objectifying and formative demands of making a novel of his autobiography brought him to peace with himself as it sketched the rationalization of the dawning age of mid-nineteenth-century America.

IV *Seduction Revisited*—Ruth Elder

One of the final reworkings of Neal's sexual trauma comes in *Ruth Elder*, a novel which ran serially during Neal's editorship of *Brother Jonathan*[24] in 1843. The literary journal was published by Edward Stephens and drew its contributors from the Down-East group of his wife Ann, Seba Smith and his wife Elizabeth Oakes Smith, and N. P. Willis. Neal was especially close that year to the former Portlanders, now members of the literary circle of New York City. He provided, for instance, the preface to Mrs. Smith's first volume of collected poems at this time.

As the duty of filling the pages of *Brother Jonathan* became his responsibility, he drew heavily on his own material. It is possible, therefore, that *Ruth Elder* had been written some years before its appearance—possibly as early as 1825 as some of the material excised from the sprawling novel that confusingly bears the same name as the journal. The setting of the novel in the Down-East regions of Maine relates it both to "Otter Bag" (which was indeed cut out as an expendable episode, to be published separately in 1829) and to his projected series of North American tales, of which the novel *Rachel Dyer* (1828) is an expanded version of one. *Ruth Elder* also has a North of Boston locale. Recent critics have tended to overlook this serial novel, however, even though Rufus Griswold in 1849 referred to it as "the last and in some respects the best of his novels."[25]

The narrator, named Page, is instructed by an old man to deliver a brooch with a picture of a tree to one Ruth Elder of Freeport, Maine. As a boy the old man had planted a tree. On his last visit, he had found it cut down and only the child Ruth had sympathized with his sorrow. On the brooch is the motto "Woodman, spare that tree!"—a sentiment that causes Page to prophesy of the day fast coming "when a large, handsome tree will be the making of a whole neighborhood" (*RE*, V, 361). This early conservationist doctrine, however, is not developed further. The story is to be one of sex and seduction. Ruth, the only child of a dead wife, is disliked by her stepmother. Page spends the night at the Elder farm and is visited in his room by the fourteen-year-old elfin Ruth, a combination of innocence and awakening womanhood that characterizes the real-life Abby and so many of Neal's fictional heroines.

Page steals a kiss just as the father stumps up the stairs. Page feigns sleep but is found out. He develops a fever and must stay several days. That night he gets Ruth to read Coleridge to him:

> 'Twas partly love, and partly fear
> And partly 'twas a bashful art
> That I might rather feel than see
> The beating of her heart.

The passage, a favorite of Neal's, had been used in his "What is Poetry?" essay, but here it is metaphor for the increasing feeling between the couple. Literature as a device of flirtation continues as Page visits Ruth's room and finds her with an Italian version of *Paul and Virginia*. She is tremendously moved by the story but suspects Page's motives: "I am afraid of you . . . you seem to know too much for an honest man" (*RE*, V, 476). She tries to avoid him but they are soon translating the scene where Virginia becomes a woman in emotions, as Ruth discovers that she is less a child than she supposed. But Page must leave. Heartbroken, Ruth wishes to go with him and see his wife. A short while later she puts her wish into action; she arrives at Page's house. There the tension between the husband's worry that his wife will misunderstand his relationship and Ruth's sometimes embarrassingly innocent actions builds on the guilt that husbands often feel. As the visit extends, the wife's jealousy begins to surface. Neal's lengthy development of this triangle suggests that at least this part of the story was written subsequently to his marriage in 1828 to Eleanor Hall—nineteen to his thirty-five years. It is significant that the wife in the story is also named Eleanor.

There now develops a most ambiguous situation. Ruth is stricken with illness, probably emotional in its causes. The wife nurses her, but her own life wanes as Ruth's strengthens. The struggle between them is at a psychic level parallel to that in Poe's "Ligeia" (1838). Page must leave on a month's trip. Ruth, not his wife, receives his farewell kiss. He returns to find Eleanor desperately ill. Her deathbed wish is for Page to marry Ruth. Suddenly the story takes a surprise turn.

With Page within her grasp, Ruth rejects the arrangement: she will have nothing secondhand. When she returns to her father's, Eleanor remarkably recovers. Ahead lies tragedy for Ruth. Her stepmother plots against her, and introduces the British seducer Ford into Ruth's bedroom. In shame she leaves home. Page runs Ford to earth in New York City, but the Britisher escapes aboard ship. The mystery of Ruth's end is left unsolved except for her final poem with its reference to her baby.

The story has been related at length because it is not discussed elsewhere, because it is today nearly inaccessible, and because it reveals a final and involved variation on the traumatic bedroom scene of Neal's early novels. There would seem to be two developments of the basic episode in the *Ruth Elder* version. The first ends with the seventh of sixteen installments: Ruth is left behind as Page returns to his wife. The second is the Ligeia-like plot that ends with Ruth's renouncement of Page at the end of installment thirteen. Both represent in differing ways Neal dealing not only with the Abby episode but also with what he called "the most disgraceful affair of my whole life,"[26] his involvement with Mrs. Howard.

Knowing her tarnished reputation, Neal sought to launch his mistress on a new life. He ultimately sent her to Boston to consult with the tragedian Cooper about a stage career, but he also had toyed with the idea of giving her asylum "in the mansion of my own mother; and give her, too, for her companion, the purity of my own sister." He had "made her love him better than aught on earth," but with more practical wisdom than Neal's she refused to enter an asylum which he called "the most sacred in the world."

Like Mrs. Howard, Ruth Elder has succumbed to a compelling love, but Neal actually takes this imagined, desperate girl into the home, not of a mother but of a wife. The change allows a distancing from his more confessional account in *Randolph* as he explores the dire results of a *ménage à trois*.[27] Before actual tragedy, however, Ruth, like Mrs. Howard, refuses the proffered escape from her fate. The ultimate and presumably fatal end remains obscure and unknown.

There is a quieter tone of greater distance to this final dealing with his own sexual affairs, unlike the heated and hectic versions in the novels of the mid-1820s when the author seemed close to emotional collapse. Just how close—in these years just prior to his sailing for England—Neal was to collapse, we may never know; but the signs of his approaching a breaking point are clear. From the ruins of his mercantile dreams, he had plunged into law and literature with a near furor. His novels of the period have a hectic flush about them. It is not merely his heroes but the author himself who now projects titanic frenzy. The two central traumas of fear of violence and of sexual adventure are dwelt on fixedly—while the line between autobiography and fiction is drawn finer and finer. His clash with Pinckney and his break with Pierpont had come at a time when he was thrown increasingly in on himself. When his friend William B. Walter was rejected for membership in the Delphian Club, Neal—who had proposed him—resigned in January, 1820. Thus he was without a social outlet at the very time that Pierpont had left for Boston and Neal was whiplashing himself into law and literature. The same year saw his successful entrance into law practice, but increasing disillusion with the law followed. [28]

Even his robust health was suffering. He found himself on the floor of his room in Baltimore in a dead faint from overwork. A second attack in London frightened him into setting a better physical regimen for himself. All in all he was suffering a personal crisis in the early 1820s—a crisis that for his fictional heroes often ended in madness. In the full development of the Abby episode, for example, in *Errata* (*E*, I, 286–325), the scene is even for Neal unusually overwrought. Will Adams and the young Caroline are caught in passionate embrace by her parents. The results are violent and tragic out of all proportion. Will falls unconscious, only to regain his senses months later in a madhouse. Caroline, next door, is dying. Gothic and sentimental rant? To some extent, possibly; but also Neal is here objectifying the struggle with his own demons. Just how much he feared madness for himself, we have no way of knowing. But he fled the scenes of trouble; in December, 1823, he set sail for England where he found a new identity as Carter Holmes, essayist and critic for *Blackwood's Magazine*.

Before this, however, Neal's self-projections convey an image of belligerence, self-confidence, and egotism. Yet much of this impression is false— a shallow reflection from the mask of defense he drew on to meet the world. Only Pierpont—until their break—had been allowed behind the facade where a sensitive, proud, and ambitious young man struggled with real problems and a few demons. In spite of an element of self-pity, the following passage is a reminder of a nearly desperate John Neal.

I was poor. I saw no likelihood of being otherwise, for many a weary year. I was but just entering a profession, perilous, and uncertain. Many years were to be spent in my novitiate, for I had no education. I was taken from school at twelve,—my mother was a widow woman,—poor, and kept a school for a living. And many years more must pass, before I ought to think of loving. What then? Was there nothing noble? Nothing of self denial? Nothing heroick, in this sacrifice? . . . Well—I returned to my home—entered upon my studies—toiled day and night, as no other man ever toiled in America. (*R*, I, 172)

The words are assigned to a fictional character, but the details are exact to the life of his creator in those difficult Baltimore days when Neal stormed the bastions of law and literature with his solitary naked strength. Escape to a new battlefield beckoned; he began 1824 in England.

CHAPTER 4

"Who Reads an American Book?"

A S the year 1823 was closing, Neal had come through the ferment and turmoil of an emotional crisis that is reflected in the three novels he published that year. Without the friendship of Pierpont and with the animosity of Pinckney, Baltimore was no longer attractive; and Neal found himself in that mood for a change in which the merest event can trigger a resolve to move on. That event came at a dinner party given by a British resident of Baltimore, Henry Robinson, who alluded to the familiar gibe of Sydney Smith, "Who reads an American book?" Neal—whose *Logan* and *Seventy-Six* had both been published in London a few months earler—would himself force a positive answer to the question. He would go to England with a case filled with his books and new manuscript; they would all read John Neal.

Within a few days, on November 15, 1823, he wrote Mathew Carey of his intent to go to London to seek publication, and thence on to Paris, and Rome.[1] Exactly a month later—on a wet, nasty day—he sailed aboard the *Franklin*. The passage was stormy; but, fighting seasickness, Neal managed to continue amassing manuscript for his new novel, ultimately to be entitled *Brother Jonathan*. Twenty-three days out of Baltimore, on January 8, 1824, the ship docked at Liverpool. In settling his affairs before departure, Neal had raised enough money to last him several months. He therefore approached London in a leisurely fashion by touring the villages along the route, arriving at Oxford on January 30, 1824. He was still keeping his sea diary, passages of which appear in his "London Forty Years Ago."

During February and March he settled into London, moving finally into rooms once occupied by Washington Irving. The hopes he had of London publication, however, were dashed when he approached the firms of Newman and Company and of the Whittakers. Each had been willing enough to pirate one of his novels, but neither

70

was interested in having to pay the American author for bringing out another of his works. With money running dangerously low, he had to find another path to survival and fame. In early April, Neal sent his first article to *Blackwood's Magazine,* presenting himself in the role of British traveler recently returned from America and signing himself Carter Holmes. While awaiting a response, Neal learned that the Whittakers were completely rejecting *Randolph.* His situation was desperate when on April 20, William Blackwood responded. He would publish Neal's article on the American presidents and candidates. Enclosed was a draft for five guineas.[2]

I   Blackwood's

Neal had planned his invasion of the British press well. His first article was timed to capitalize on public interest in the recently announced Monroe Doctrine. As he sketched the five presidential candidates—Jackson, J. Q. Adams, Clay, Calhoun, and Crawford— he demonstrated, at the very time of the opening of the campaign of 1824, how American policy reflected personal characteristics of each president. Appearing in *Blackwood's* in May, 1824, the article was widely quoted and was republished as a totality in the *New European,* which had a Continental circulation.

In launching his magazine career, Neal had deliberately selected *Blackwood's Edinburgh Magazine* as the most original and trend-setting of the periodicals, and it was a fortunate choice. The editor John Wilson—famous as "Christopher North"—had talents similar to Neal's[3] and so might be expected to respond favorably to Neal's brash and sometimes undisciplined talent. Neal, the descendant of a royalist Scot, might find a place among the Edinburgh journalists. Further, the publisher, William Blackwood, was always looking for the new and startling; his review had captured the lead among British magazines by a reputation for novelty, and certainly the new disguised American had that. Blackwood was also hospitable to any writer who exhibited "natural" or unschooled genius. For example, the shepherd poet James Hogg had been associated with the magazine for some time, but a recent falling out left a void that Neal could fill. Also recently the magazine had shown an increased interest in the Yankee, a topic upon which Neal was an expert. His tone, moreover, of contentious strong opinion and his avowed aesthetic based on Schlegel's doctrine of effect were shared with Blackwood, Wilson, and their magazine. Neal found himself warmly welcomed and handsomely paid; he set himself to rapid production. From July,

1824, to February, 1826, he had an article in every issue of *Blackwood's*. [4]

Traits already apparent in Neal's writing came to the fore during his association with *Blackwood's:* contentiousness as a means of forcing public attention, rhetorical tricks like the insultingly mistaken name ("Wirt or Wart"), devastating lists of grammatical errors found in the writing of opponents, a self-assured attitude of being the guardian of quality, and exploitation of the personal by projecting a Byronic personality. All of these traits were shared by Neal and the Edinburgh magazine. [5]

But his articles were not mere journalistic trickery. The substance of his reviews of American writers and artists is sound, indeed remarkable, since he had to depend almost wholly upon memory. In effect, he wrote the first history of American literature in his articles that appeared serially through 1824 and 1825. While he is unfair to Cooper and gives the largest space to himself, his critical acumen is brilliant. Fred Lewis Pattee finds that ". . . his critical judgments have held. Where he condemned, time has almost without exception condemned also. He had that rarest of powers, critical vision." [6] His opinions were widely quoted in England and did bring about a change in knowledge concerning the new United States of North America, as Neal liked to refer to his country. There is little question that he succeeded in an unprecedented way. Robert Spiller, who studied the role of Americans in England in the early nineteenth century, concludes that "Neal's story is unique. He accomplished what he had set out to do. . . ." But then Spiller dashes this praise by continuing, "but it may be feared that he added one caricature to England's gallery of American portraits. . . ."[7] Neal's success story was in fact soon to turn sour. Not content to be the first American to join the ranks of top British literary journalists, he must appear as a major novelist. He submitted to Blackwood's publishing firm his new and lengthy *Brother Jonathan.* While they would eventually bring it out in a toned down version, the submission brought a change in Neal's fortunes for the worse.

II   Brother Jonathan

From the time he had subdued the sexuality of *Keep Cool* at the urging of Pierpont, Neal's fiction had always been more explicit about the passions than was usual for the times. As an American Byron, he was true to his model, combining his own devils of passion with literary dramatization of them. The same blend is evident in the new long novel that he carried to England; and it was judged in its first form to be by far too outspoken. The publisher's readers had the same reaction as a reviewer of *Randolph:* Neal presents "a daring and naked exposure of what people in general, cannot avoid *thinking,* but dare not express."[8] Neal in his new novel still dared to express too much female sexuality and male profligacy for the taste of William Blackwood to whom he submitted it: ". . . it is not fit for young people to read of seduction, brothels, and the abandoned of both sexes . . ." wrote the Scottish publisher.[9] Revision was in order and Neal set to work, excising digressive stories such as "Otter-Bag" and subduing explicit scenes of passion. The result still troubled Blackwood who asked for further revision, but even after Neal's further attempts to comply, the final version ran to a prolix three volumes totaling some thirteen hundred pages of disturbing material.

The title of this longest of Neal's books, *Brother Jonathan,* was well chosen for the author's purpose of thrusting upon the British attention the unique qualities of Yankeeism that he himself and his novel illustrate. Originally a nickname of derision applied by the British to an American patriot, "Brother Jonathan" had been accepted and then flaunted as the personification of a citizen of America. Not until the 1830s was Uncle Sam to rival Brother Jonathan as the national symbol.[10]

Neal's hope to capture a reading public in England and thus to invalidate Sydney Smith's sneer rested on this, his most ambitious book. Against his spirit and his professed beliefs in spontaneous writing, he had rewritten the manuscript three times before the firm of Blackwood agreed to publish it. The author received a generous two hundred guineas upon publication—delivered in person by William Blackwood. Another one hundred were due when one thousand copies had been sold, but alas, the initial printing of two thousand moved slowly. The firm suffered loss with a sale of only five hundred copies; misunderstandings arose on both sides and the relationship of Neal with the Edinburgh publishers strained and broke.

The problem with the novel was one of focus. Brilliant yet exasperating, *Brother Jonathan* was many things, but no one thing for long. To this day, critics read it differently. To Lease, it is a story of initiation of young Walter Harwood during the eve of the Revolution. To Cowie, the protagonist is not Harwood but the Byronic Jonathan Peters, while Martin and Menner treat the novel as a regional source book on Yankee dialect and folklore.[11] No wonder that the reading public did not know what to make of the sprawling, brawling work, and ended by ignoring it. In a sense, all the critics are correct in their interpretations, but it is Lease who comes closest to Neal's intent. It was supposed to be Walter's story, but the mysterious Peters—another of Neal's titans—introduces so much melodrama and gothicism that Walter fades. Blaming revision instead of his own lack of artistic control, Neal wrote to Blackwood, "Deuse take Brother Jonathan. Peters would have made a capital hero; but—but—I did not think of him, in that shape, till it was too late, and I was weary of the work."[12] Neal's afterthought would not have improved the novel, but he did sense the fatal flaw. He had the kind of outpouring talent of a certain type of American writer; his flood of words contained much that sparkled but also much that was muddied and roiled. Like the later Thomas Wolfe, Neal needed a creative editor; but he never found his Maxwell Perkins. Each reader, as it were, is therefore forced to select and "write" his own version out of the richly laden raw material. Few readers are willing to make the effort.

Following Lease, one may trace the adventures of the young New Englander Walter Harwood during the first year of the American Revolution. As a frontier innocent in love with Edith, another child of nature, Walter travels to New York through a countryside gearing up for war. He experiences vicissitudes of nature and fallen human nature as he seeks to join General Washington's forces. In New York City he encounters the grimier aspects of life, is led to a house of prostitution, and meets the seductive Mrs. P. He finds other girls susceptible to his fresh country charms, and undergoes a baptism of war at Brooklyn Heights, followed by an encounter with Nathan Hale. Walter escapes as Hale is hanged. From there on the gothic elements introduced by Peters engulf Walter's story. Walter himself develops some of the libertine titanism of Peters, has an affair with Emma (out of jealousy over Peters' attention to his true love Edith), rejects Emma, but returns to her when she bears his child. They part when the child dies, and Walter is thus saved from a sordid liaison in order to eventually win fair Edith, but only when he returns to the better world of the New England coast. Walter's initiation into the city, war, and passion has awakened the sleeping genius in him. His change is marked by his boyish Yankee dialect becoming the speech of "genius."[13]

Such a summary of *Brother Jonathan,* however, neglects the very real social history it contains. Customs such as huskings, wrestling matches, barn raisings, town meetings, quilting parties, suppers with "long and short sarse," doughnuts, and Indian puddings fill the early pages (*BJ*, I, chap. 3, for example). Further, the story incorporates some of the best of Neal's attempts at exact recording of American dialect, a facet properly stressed by Menner and Martin. With linguistic virtuosity, Neal contrasts the speechways of Walter's New England with those of Edith's Virginia: her talk is spiced with expressions such as "I reckon," "jest," "mighty bad," "leave me be." When teased, she defends her speech by noting that "We all *say* that, which none of us would *write*"—a clear expression of Neal's theory of capturing actual talk on paper. Examples of New England speech are carefully scored; accent marks and italics are used to indicate rhythm, and attempts are made to describe pitch and tone (*BJ*, I, 13–15). The Negro speech of a Georgia runaway occurs (*BJ*, II, 296) as do extended examples of the Indian speech of Bald Eagle, whose "carriage of the indolent young Greek" marks him as one of nature's noblemen (*BJ*, II, chap. 14; I, 283). Even the Quaker idiosyncrasies of Hannah Grizzle, a "she-preacher," are set forth (*BJ*, II, 164). From such details of language and folkways the British readers could have gleaned an accurate picture of America, but the gothic vehicle overwhelmed the social history. And Neal's full-blooded women were found offensive.

When Walter succumbs to the profligate ways of a friend, he learns to prefer the good bad-girl to the conventional heroine: he comes to dislike "good" girls as "fat, lazy good-humoured females, who shuffle through the serious duties of life . . . (*BJ*, II, 340). And he defends the outcast because ". . . women fall, not because of their being worse—but because of their being better, than usual" (*BJ*, II, 298).

For such ungentlemanly truth about women as well as the formlessness of the novel, Neal's "major" work was a failure. He came to realize that in straining after originality, he had fallen into romantic excess. In a letter to Blackwood, he confessed,

I, wishing to avoid what is common, am apt to run off into what is not only uncommon, but unnatural, and even absurd. I am aware of this, and would have corrected it, long before this, were I not afraid of uprooting some valuable characteristick of my own, while tearing up the roots of that which I acknowledge to be vicious.[14]

In giving free rein to his genius, he had run to excess by straining after effect.

Neal had now been in England for nearly two years. His assault through the magazines had succeeded; but *Brother Jonathan,* which was to establish his reputation as a major author, was stillborn, a monster birth. By quarreling with *Blackwood's,* he lost his best market and was at a dead end. To the query "Who reads an American book?" the answer was a mere five hundred who bought *Brother Jonathan.* The American was once more adrift in Britain when he met Jeremy Bentham.

III   *Jeremy Bentham*

To one of John Neal's boundless energy and considerable talents, difficulties only served as challenge. Whatever his discouragement in the fall of 1825, Neal never let on, then or later, that he was concerned. He threw off articles for most of the London magazines, finding them, however, less generous in payment than *Blackwood's.* He needed a new line of endeavor, and it came to him through a debating society of young university graduates. He harangued the society on women's rights and other reform topics that were tinged with utilitarianism. The group included, as it turned out, a number who were working closely with Jeremy Bentham. Through them, Neal was invited to dine with the great man. Although Neal was then residing only a few hundred yards from Bentham's Hermitage, he had not before found his way down the cul-de-sac to the small courtyard set with shrubs where Bentham lived and worked with the Mills, father and son, his translator Etienne Dumont, his editor-secretary John Bowring, and John Austin. The establishment was a physical and intellectual "oasis in the desert,"[15] and so it proved to Neal for a time.

At dinner the outspoken and argumentative American lawyer-writer impressed Bentham sufficiently that by January, 1826, he was invited to take up the rooms at the Hermitage once occupied by America's earliest utilitarian, Aaron Burr.[16] Neal's interest in Bentham went back to the time he was studying law in Baltimore. He had been aroused to the new ideas by Professor David Hoffman of the University of Maryland, whose considerable library was put at Neal's disposal. Hoffman had suggested the need of a translation of Bentham's French works, and Neal projected a translation of Dumont's version of the *Principles of Legislation.* At that time he failed of interesting a publisher, but now he reembarked on the project.[17]

In his long introduction to the translation, Neal discusses why Bentham wrote in French, but the discussion reveals a good deal about the agony that Neal experienced in revising his novel at

Blackwood's behest. Bentham had stated that he wrote in a foreign language because he was less aware of its pitfalls than he was in his native English. Neal elaborates:

Many will never understand this; but they who have gone over and over the same page, sounding it aloud as it were in the very depths of their hearts, sentence by sentence, till they are fritted through every fibre with a fever that cannot be soothed; till they shrink with a diseased nerve, and a childish, though preternatural anxiety, at every jar in the smooth ringing of their words, unable to endure the clashing of un-pronounceable consonants, and casting about their language, into every variety of shape, to avoid the union of ds, or ts with ts, or vs with fs, or any two letters of the same or a similar sound with each other—all . . . [such] will understand and pity the nervousness that drove Jeremy Bentham to write in a foreign language [18]

The passage is remarkable for the insight into Neal as a conscious artist, for his usual public stance was as a slapdash writer who never revised. But clearly he spoke from his own knowledge of the pains of revision.

For nearly a year and a half Neal lived in the Bentham household, while he projected his New England tales, of which *Rachel Dyer* became an expanded version of one, and wrote for Bentham's *Westminster Review*. His temperament, though, was sadly unsuited to the climate of rivalries that surrounded Bentham; and he was soon a storm center. He fought with a housekeeper and managed to get her banished. Tensions with John Stuart Mill and John Bowring were, however, more damaging to his relationship with their patron. Trouble broke into the open over an article that Bentham had asked Neal to write for the *Westminster*. Without Neal's knowledge, Bowring as editor inserted his own comments into Neal's article; the offending paragraph was highly detrimental to Neal's position on American literature and served to embarrass him for years to come. The Bowring attack on American writers, reads

Violent exaggeration is the character of American literature at the present day, and compared with the chaster and more rational style of our best writers, the style of the North American authors is usually the rant and unmeaning vehemence of a strolling Thespian, when placed beside the calm, appropriate, and expressive delivery of an accomplished actor. [19]

Perhaps Bowring meant to chasten Neal by a criticism that applied all too well to *Brother Jonathan*, but Neal never forgave him. Passages in *Wandering Recollections*, years later, still try to pillory Bowring.

By the spring of 1827, Neal was thinking of moving on, and there is no indication that Bentham was sorry to see the last of his brilliant but difficult American. When Neal applied for funds to finance a trip to the Continent, Bentham refused; but did offer to pay passage back to America where he felt Neal's talent would find a better arena. On April 14, 1827, Neal left England, managing to eke out a month in Paris and environs before taking ship for New York. He landed in June, intending to enter the magazine editing business and ordering his stored library to be shipped from Baltimore. A visit home to see his mother and sister, however, became the long visit of a lifetime. He found the New England press against him and popular sentiment believing that in Britain he had defamed America to gain personal advantages. A faction in Portland wanted him out of town. With typical perversity, he would stay just because they dared to tell him what he could or could not do. He would enter the Maine bar and edit a utilitarian journal in Portland. He had come home to stay.

CHAPTER 5

New England Fiction

IN his first years back in Portland, John Neal published three
novels: *Rachel Dyer* (1828), *Authorship* (1830), and *The Down-
Easters* (1833); one play, *Our Ephraim* (1835); and a series of tales. In
each genre he makes use of the New England setting that he knew so
well. The first novel reaches into colonial history for the material of
the Salem witchcraft delusion. Written with better control than his
prior works of fiction, *Rachel Dyer* is quite readable today. *Authorship* in its autobiographical self-justification more nearly resembles
his earlier novels, while *The Down-Easters,* although structurally
flawed, is thoroughly entertaining. As a spin-off of the last novel, the
play *Our Ephraim* captures Yankee dialect with wit and accuracy; and
the tales combine locale with psychological depth.

I Rachel Dyer

Rachel Dyer is a carefully documented tale based upon the fortunes
of George Burroughs, an irregular preacher who had for a time been
at Falmouth, later Portland. This local connection may have been
Neal's incentive in taking up the tale, but his own open-mindedness
about the possibilities of communication with the spirit world[1] may
also have led to his reading about witchcraft. [2] Still further, as a lawyer
he would have been drawn to the old court records of the Salem trials
at a time when his own persecution in Portland created sympathy
with Burroughs. Whatever the initial impulse, he first had prepared
the story of the Quakeress Rachel Dyer and her friend George
Burroughs for *Blackwood's Magazine,* but by one of those misunderstandings that came easily to one of Neal's turbulent character he
had withdrawn the manuscript. The novel is thus an expansion and
revision of the earlier tale, and shows in its greater control the mature
reworking of the author. This is a rare quality in Neal, who nearly
always wrote at white heat. Indeed, there was a second reason for the
extraordinary care he gave this work. In his first year back in

Portland, he was on his good behavior, determined to rewin the respect he had lost by his outspoken articles on America in the English journals. *The Yankee,* which he edited through 1828 and 1829, sought to justify Neal to his countrymen, and *Authorship* in 1828, is less of a novel than a combination apologia and travelogue. In 1828, using the material he had at hand, Neal published *Rachel Dyer* with the same purpose, hoping that "it may be regarded by the wise and virtuous of our country as some sort of atonement for the folly and extravagance of my earlier writing."[3] By way of further justification he included with the novel an "Unpublished Preface" that was to have accompanied the original tale in *Blackwood's.* This preface elaborates on Neal's reaction to the query, "Who reads an American book?"—a query which had taken him on his one-man mission to England—and his answer is a call for "another Declaration of Independence, in the great *Republic of Letters.*" He recalls how he dreamed of being an author, ". . . a dream of my boyhood, indefinite, vague and shadowy. . . ." Fired by personal desire and native pride, he concluded that "to succeed the American author must *resemble* nobody." Thus he developed his own style and cultivated his eccentricities until he could conclude, "I have the modesty to believe that in some things I am unlike all the other writers of my country—both living and dead." Now he will present a novel that will show his countrymen that "there are abundant and hidden sources of fertility in their own beautiful brave earth . . ." and also show the English what an American author can do.[4]

The resulting novel is one of Neal's best written, but for all its calmer style, *Rachel Dyer* is marked in two respects as the work of John Neal: the titanism of Burroughs and the deformity of the heroine, Rachel. In *Errata* (1823) Neal had presented the dwarf Hammond as "a creature of great moral beauty and strength," in order to prove the falsity of novelists who felt that personal beauty and moral beauty are inseparably connected. Now in making the hump-backed, red-freckled Rachel his heroine, Neal was returning to this favorite idea. He correctly credits Godwin with perceiving this truth and finds in Brown, Scott, and Byron "that a towering intellect may inhabit a miserable body," but contends that by making their titans into villains, or at best outlaws, these writers obscured what Neal wanted to be irrefutably illustrated.[5] And so he couples great energy with great goodness, and directs the titanism of his own heroes into virtuous paths; since their principles are right, they act for the best, even when opposing the law, which may be inhumanly rigid. George Burroughs, like Copely and Archibald in *Seventy-Six*, Molton in *Randolph*, and Hammond in *Errata*, is a fusion of the Byronic superman with Neal's projection of his own energy, iconoclasm, and revolt. These violent figures are more than literary puppets to Neal; they are his heroic ideals personified. But it was one thing to have titanic heroes, even a deformed titan like Hammond; and quite another to furnish the titan with a heroine of the same proportions. Yet this is what Neal now does, for he writes "If God ever made a heroine, Rachel Dyer was a heroine—a heroine without youth or beauty, with no shape to please, with no color to charm the eye, with no voice to delight the ear" (*RD*, 148). In an age of sentimental paragons, it is testimony of Neal's power that he was able to make the reader believe in Rachel's genuine beauty of the soul and spirit.

It is not for the romantic doctrine of the titan, however Neal worked it out, that *Rachel Dyer* is readable today, but for the vivid, dramatic re-creations of the trial scenes at Salem. As a lawyer and novelist Neal had the two talents needed to shake the dust from the old court records and to revitalize the emotions and passions that had been dried out by law jargon.[6] As Burroughs pleads for the life of a foolish old woman about to be sentenced for witchcraft, Neal is able through his hero's mouth to present his own liberal views. He can expose the injustice of the old laws with their requirement that the burden of the proof be placed on the accused in establishing his innocence, and with their inequality in letting the state subpoena witnesses while denying this right to the accused. In a Federalist town, Neal had no longing for the "good old days"; republican America was much preferable to the America of crown colonies, and the principle that proved this was "that where human life is thought much of, there liberty is; and that just in proportion to the value of human life are the number and variety, the greatness and the strength of the safe-guards forms and ceremonies [*sic*], which go to make it secure, if not altogether inaccessible" (*RD*, 104).

This was not the first or last time that Neal was to use fiction as a vehicle for his opinions, for all his novels are built around some point he wishes to make. *Keep Cool* (1817) had been written to discourage duelling, a crusade that he adopted from Godwin and was to return to in his self-defensive *Errata* (1823). *Seventy-Six* rewrote history in terms of the theory that great times produce great men.[7] And there were frequent side issues, such as his defense of King Philip, the Indian warrior (*RD*, 38–40); his constant preaching of literary

nationalism; and his digressions into essays on literature and art, as in
Randolph. Issues of law reform, imbibed from Bentham, give theme
to *Rachel Dyer*.

   While *Rachel Dyer* is not—as claimed by Leisy—the first American novel to treat witchcraft in New England,[8] it is the first hardcover
novel to center on the Salem events. The only true predecessor was
the anonymous *Salem, an Eastern Tale* which had run serially in 1820
in a New York journal, but distribution was small and influence
smaller.[9] In contrast, Neal's example helped to stimulate Whittier's
use of witchcraft in a number of poems and in the prose "The Haunted
House" and "The Pow-waw,"[10] which appeared in his *Legends of
New England* (1831). Perhaps Hawthorne's omission of any writing
directly on the Salem outbreak and his ancestor's role in the trials
arose from a feeling that Neal had preempted the topic. Also among
the northern New England writers, Longfellow treated witchcraft,
publishing as late as 1868 his *New England Tragedies*.

   Neal's novel was suggestive to these younger writers in a number of
ways. He established the woods as a gothic abode of the devil (*RD*,
48), stressed the effects of solitude on the superstitious nature of a
"man living away and apart from all that he knew, on the very
outskirts of the solitude . . . " (*RD*, 51), and pioneered in symbolism
that must have struck Hawthorne's imagination. Thus, the child
Bridget Pope looks up from her slate to view her Salem village nearly
swallowed up by

a part of the original woods of North America—huge trees that were found
there on the first arrival of the white man crowded together and covered with
moss and dropping to pieces with age; a meeting house with a short wooden
spire, and the figure of death on the top for a weathercock, a multitude of
cottages that appeared to be lost in landscape. . . . (*RD*, 53)

A symbolic death's head looks down on the isolated village in
premonition of the events soon to follow.

   The representation of the children Bridget and Abby is particularly
well done as Neal develops them from prank-playing outdoor children into neurotic and frightened creatures in the grip of witchcraft
(*RD*, 54–5, 196). Hawthorne may also have been influenced by Neal's
effectively dramatic gallows scene where Sarah Good curses her
tormentors:

Believe ye that a mortal woman of my age, with a rope about her neck, hath
power to prophesy? If ye do, give ear to my speech and remember my words.

For death, ye shall have death! For blood, ye shall have blood—blood on the earth! blood in the sky! blood in the waters! Ye shall drink blood and breathe blood, you and yours, for the work of this day! (*RD*, 62–63)

Echoes of Sarah's curse stream in the portentous sky of *The Scarlet Letter* and in Maule's curse of *The House of Seven Gables*. This curse is uttered near the end of Chapter 4. The earlier chapters had provided a slow, historical entrance to the novel. The tone is there scholarly and quiet, making all the more dramatic this scene of the hanging. And it is at this exciting moment that the delayed entrance of the heroine Rachel Dyer takes place.

From this point on, the pace of the novel shifts, with the story carried by heavy use of dialogue handled with Neal's maturest control. Without labels, he is able to keep the characters straight and to present them effectively "talking on paper." (See *RD*, 75–82, 210–219 as well as all of chapter 17, for examples.) This dialogue also includes some good Yankee dialect (*RD*, 160–162) of the sort to be exploited in his next novel. In fact, the hero Burroughs is one part Byron, one part Neal (whose recent reception in Portland gave him sympathy with the misunderstood and persecuted Burroughs), and one part Yankee frontiersman of superior strength, native woodcraft, and frontier rhetoric. His swarthy complexion reveals his partial Indian blood, making him for Neal a doubly patriotic incarnation of noble American struggling against the tyranny of British law.

In presenting the growing mood of hysteria that will lead to the execution of Burroughs and the death of Rachel, Neal shows acute understanding of why belief in witchcraft was a part of seventeenth-century life. His authorities include not only Cotton Mather, but Blackstone, Samuel Johnson, Byron, and Bentham, all of whom shared a belief in ghosts. A notable passage of several pages reveals sympathy for the deluded as well as for the persecuted. It commences:

We may smile now to hear witchcraft spoken seriously of; but we forget perhaps that a belief in it is like a belief in the after appearance of the dead among the blue waters, the green graves, the still starry atmosphere and the great shadowy woods of our earth; or like the beautiful deep instinct of our nature for worship. . . . (*RD*, 22)

Rooted thus in their very religious views and stimulated by the isolation of Salem in the primeval forest, belief in the supernatural caught up young and old, even when it became a vehicle of private revenge as it ultimately did. Testimony against Burroughs comes from Judith Hubbard, "a woman whose character had been at his mercy for a long while (He knew that of her, which if he had revealed it before she accused him, would have been fatal to her) . . ." (RD, 220). She who had once loved him and then injured him draws her revenge from sexual frustration, a cause today more readily attributed to the witchcraft hysteria than when Neal wrote in 1828.

In such interpretation of history, as well as in its careful control, its good realization of dialogue and controlled dialect, and its warm sympathy for the characters, *Rachel Dyer* is one of the very best of Neal's works of fiction. In it he demonstrated what he claimed in the "Unpublished Preface," "that there are abundant and hidden sources of fertility in our own [that is, American] beautiful earth, waiting only to be broken up . . ." (RD, xvi).

II Authorship

Between his historical novel of the American colonial past, *Rachel Dyer,* and his contemporary social comedy of *The Down-Easters,* Neal published in 1830 a sprightly spoof upon his own and others' pretentions. Tone and content of this novel, *Authorship,*[11] relate it closely to the novels of his Baltimore period with their confounding of fact and fancy. Indeed, the bulk of *Authorship* had probably been written while he was resident in the household of Jeremy Bentham. Some of the wit and satire seems to reflect that circle of the young men around Bentham; and its viewpoint of an American author abroad as set out on the title page, "By a New Englander Over-Sea," clearly fits the earlier period. The plot—what there is of it—is sentimental romance, but with less of the gothic trappings and mystery that obscure his Baltimore novels.

In fact, the relative absence of plot is a blessing as Neal presents an American eye-view of British scenes. Long before Twain, Neal offers refreshing correctives to literary Anglophiles who went to England, like Irving, only to admire. Neal himself is thinly disguised as an author-narrator Carter Holmes (his own pseudonym with Blackwood), who goes abroad to see "much there, that I hope never to see in America, much that I do hope to see here" (A, 1). Westminster Abbey, a sentimental shrine to Irving, is not one of the latter:

Others may be able to see more—especially if they go to the Abbey when it is getting dark. . . . But as I live, though I paid my sixpence at the door, and my eighteen-pence after I got into the church, and although I took off my hat, and particularly desired to see every thing—I did not see a fortieth part of what I expected to see, after reading the Sketch-Book and The Quarterly Review. (A, 3)

He sees no spectres of a storied past but a very real couple in apparent assignation. In the dim religious light, he has "unholy thoughts," for he will tell the truth of his experiences at all costs. The narrator falls in love at sight with the woman and spends three years looking for her in crowds and public places.

In the meantime he compares Europe and America. The contrast of landscapes—a natural presentation of the difference between the beautiful and the sublime—strikes him: the English scenes ". . . had a beauty of their own, a beauty that we never see in the New World, a sort of pomp which is not the pomp of the wilderness. . . ." The Old World is more picturesque than the savage North American landscapes that "would startle and scare you if they were painted with fidelity" (A, 15). Even amid scenes of natural beauty, the narrator still dreams of his woman, conjuring up the grand sight of "proud woman deeply, desperately, irretrievably in love" (A, 19). He observes that for a man to enjoy nature he must have with him not Wordsworth's sister but a woman with whom he is just enough in love to "see and feel the beauty and power of solitude" (A, 25). Conversely, he confesses the real misery of one who is accompanied by a woman for whom he does not care.

Un-Irvingesque is his observation of the generally bad service at English inns. Testing the rough sheets of a hot garret room, he hopes that the Cockney maid is correct when she claims that the sheets are not "haired" (A, 47). He still cannot resist a beckoning pun,[12] but in other ways he has been sobered by his years in England; he has gained insight into himself. On his quarrelsomeness, he can now remark, "It would be foolish in me, though characteristic enough," to pick a fight over a fancied injury (A, 67). The same sort of objective self-criticism is given to Mary (or Maria as she is alternately called), his mysterious love; she is familiar with the narrator's work (that is, Neal's) and writes him some telling criticism: "Take care of that delicate line which divides the terrible from the disgusting, the sublime from the inflated, the familiar from the vulgar, the I know-not-what that is lovely, touching, and sincere in what you say about women, from what makes their cheeks tingle and their eyes quail . . ." (A, 217). Urging more restraint upon him, she advises, "Don't launch your thunder at butterflies and gnats" (A, 214). Equally telling with her criticism of Neal's writing is his presentation of the tyranny of editors and the misery of hackwork authors subjected to them (A, 105–6).

The narrator meets the couple again on the Isle of Wight where her husband identifies himself as Colonel Peter Piper and then as a variety of Neal's fictional heroes—Molton, Echo, Randolph. Both this husband—finally revealed as Edwards—and his wife are thoroughly familiar with the narrator and his works. As tragedy threatens Edwards, Mary recounts her life history as a story within a story (A, 174–178). Cursed with beauty and fine carriage, she grew up hated by her mother and distrustful of her father's pride in her. Her mother felt her to be too free with young men. None saw that her haughty bearing masked timidity, as she embarked on a search for the love she lacked at home. After a disastrous love affair, she sought peace in her marriage. Upon the narrator she leaves the impression of one who had "the courage and thought of a man, the heart and the look of a beautiful, high-spirited superior woman, the tricks of a child . . ." (A, 110). Her story occasions remarks on the problems of women as they are educated and "turned over to their husbands by their foolish mothers, in a pitiable state of delusion" (A, 180). When the narrator also notes how men fear intelligent and capable women, especially those who write, Mary responds by defending the rights of a woman to pursue a career (A, 208–10).

For a time the narrator lives and travels with the couple in an emotionally tangled *ménage à trois*. Like the wife in *Ruth Elder* but in reverse, the husband "bequeaths" his wife to Holmes, ambiguously urges him to kiss her in friendship, and often leaves them together. This rare nineteenth-century treatment of a man's love for a married woman caused Whittier, who had praised *Rachel Dyer*, to brand this novel as "not a good book."[13]

The curious blend of fact with fiction marks the book as an author's private writing, to be fully enjoyed by the few in the know. Yet, available to all is the double tone of mock seriousness that is here carried off with consistency well beyond the early attempts in *Keep Cool*. Puncturing pretentions and foibles, his own as well as those of others, the author-narrator maintains a balance between the serious and the comic: in argument with an English society critic, the American author concludes, "I never could make out whether he was laughing at me, or I at him." Such playfulness, when coupled with private jokes and the public scandal of the love story, failed to find a sufficiently sophisticated audience and the novel was hardly a success. Popular judgment survives, for a contemporary hand has written in the copy of *Authorship* in the Princeton University Library, "John Neal in this work is completely at home, his surpassing genius occasionally bursts forth from the heaps of rubbish in which he is so fond of obscuring it."

III   The Down-Easters

Three years later, Neal had contracted for a two-volume novel with Harper of New York. The germ of the novel was a sketch of incidents on board a steamboat; Neal had published it—without payment, he complained—in a short-lived New York literary journal in 1830.[14] His interest in Yankee character and dialect reached back still further, for minor Yankee figures had appeared in *Seventy-Six*. Now he let the minor figures take center stage, hoping to ride on the budding success of frontier humor as typified by his fellow townsman Seba Smith, whose Jack Downing letters were appearing in a Portland paper. Further, the popularity of Yankee plays, acted by such players as James H. Hackett and G. H. Hill, was on the immediate horizon. But Neal had the wrong vehicle for native humor. His basic plot remained that of the sentimental-gothic novel of the preceding decades, and Yankee realism and gothicism are in his ill-mixed product oil and water.

By the second volume, the gothic has taken over as Neal lifts sensationalism to new heights. In some ways—but without the latter's artistry—elements look foward to the tales of Poe.[15] The Byronic villain Gerard has been lured to a secluded house in a blasted wood. Strange clouds play overhead as he approaches it to keep an assignation, and the form of his hated enemy looms through the mist but disappears. Unearthly sounds pervade the scene as the demonic Claire leads him to the darkened chamber where waits an unknown girl. There in the chamber is enacted a terrible scene of lust, suicide, necrophilia, and revenge from which Gerard emerges a shattered man. But this is not Poe's story; Neal solves the mystery in traditional fashion with a letter from the dead girl, and all the supernatural happenings are explained *ex post facto* as natural phenomena. In its feeble conclusion the scene belongs to the method of Mrs. Radcliffe, not Poe.

The novel is a hodgepodge of un-unified and disparate sections. Whereas the last half of *The Down-Easters* is a gothic novel conveying Godwinian ethics, the first volume is a sociological study in Yankee characteristics, mannerisms, and folkways. As such it is penetrating, accurate, and amusing. The plot is a mere swindling anecdote expanded in all directions by details of character. In this, as well as in the setting aboard a steamboat, it may have provided suggestions to Herman Melville for his novel of Mississippi steamboat types, *The Confidence Man* (1857). By bringing together on one boat Yankees and Kentuckians, Northerners and Southerners, Neal is able to give a cross section of American manners, and to provide the fun of frontier humor. This was a vein he had mined as early as 1823 when he had Hammond accosted by a West Virginian in the exaggerated boasts of the West:

"By Gaud!" said the fellow. . . . "gee us your hand. . . . Do *you* know *what* I am? Steamboat!—run agin me, run agin a snag. . . . Jam up . . . got the best jack-knife, prettiest sister, best wife, run faster, jump higher, and whip any man in all Kentuck, by Gaud!" . . .
    "Come," said he, "come out, if you are a man. . . . rough and tumble." (*E*, II, 175)

Such early use of frontier braggartism as well as Neal's creation of Yankee "characters" may have influenced the Portland writer Seba Smith in the development of his Major Jack Downing.
    Yankee habits of answering a question with another question, of sharp dealing in swaps, of selling quack medicines, of holding prejudice against the Southerners, all are presented and are couched in accurate idiom to the extent that Harold C. Martin finds the novel a summary and completion of Neal's experiments in fiction, rendering it a veritable storehouse for students of dialect.[16] But as a whole, the work is a disaster. The gothic ending—Elizabeth takes a slow poison in order to die at the moment when Middleton makes love to her—abruptly ends the novel with half a volume to go. Neal refuses to carry the plot further, filling the remaining pages with two tales. The resulting potpourri appeared in an edition of fifteen hundred copies in the same year that Harper brought out a pirated edition of Jack Downing and a book on Davey Crockett.[17]
    The frontier material was the heart of the book, and had Neal stopped with the end of volume one, the result would have been a gain in unity and power. As so often, he saw more clearly what was needed than he was able to execute. His "Preface" had noted the rapid loss of regional peculiarities. With his interest in real spoken language, he inevitably wished to see speechways preserved. Fifty years after Independence, he still sees few writers of the true

American language, and hopes this novel will show the way: "Something I have accomplished here; and more I *may* attempt hereafter, should I have time for pursuing the experiment, and preparing the way for a change; but the chief work and the glory must be left to others; to the younger and more enthusiastic, with a longer life before them" (*D*, I, vi). Others will follow and he is content to let them have the final success. He will write no further novel until 1856, but he will make one more experiment in Yankee dialect, this time in a play.

IV   Our Ephraim

The literary vogue of the Yankee[18] had reached London while Neal was still resident in the Bentham household. He was, on the whole, unpleased by stage Yankees, taking special exception to the portrayal of American comic types by the British actor Charles Mathews.[19] Just before his departure, however, he found that the acting of the American James H. Hackett at Covent Garden gave a more faithful representation of Down-East characteristics; in his last days in London he befriended the young actor.[20] Some years later, back in their own country, they were to be drawn together once more. Meanwhile, Neal, back in Portland, continued his interest in the theater through reviews in *The Yankee* during 1828.

Two companies of players were competing that summer in the northern capital. John Mestayer from the Tremont Theatre of Boston had arrived in May with his group, to be overshadowed in June by Moses J. Phillips with a large cast and grandiose ideas. As Phillips spent heavily for advertisements in *The Eastern Argus*, Mestayer saw his attendance dwindling. He tried, unwisely, to get a plug from John Neal and his weekly *Yankee*. He little knew Neal's irascibility or he would not have sent one of the boys of his company with a complimentary box ticket and a ready-written puff. Neal reacted typically: "As the lad probably knew no better, I did not throw it in his face [but said], No. . . . I take no puffs from anybody . . . I puff nobody . . . for love or money. But I will pop in and look at you. . . ."[21]

Neal's interest in the local theater had been aroused. Pop in, he did at the performances of both companies, afterwards filling the summer issues of his journal with sympathetic but often severe comments. Unfortunately, his outspoken opinions aroused the enmity of the players; and he received warning that the actors intended to flog him on the streets. His response was to hurl defiance at the theater, making a special point to walk slowly past Union Hall "six times a day." One actor, whom Neal had neglected to mention at all in his reviews, became so threatening that the critic felt obliged to bind him over by law to good behavior. [22]

By the end of the season, which closed with *The Merchant of Venice* on August 8, Neal had so forgotten his war with the theater as to give a fair summary. The town's morals, he discovered had not suffered, and the bearing of the companies had been "exceedingly creditable to them." What probably pleased him most was that they had "tried to improve where criticized." [23] In his dramatic review, Neal struck a blow for a more native dramatic literature. He took occasion to complain of American dependence on England for both actors and plays. The time, he urged, was ripe for experimentation toward a new national drama, "founded altogether upon the incidents and business of republican, everyday life." [24] He was not to be disappointed, for succeeding seasons saw increasing performances of American plays and actors in Portland.

The New Theater was erected in 1830 at a cost of ten thousand dollars. The following year Edwin Forrest starred there in Indian roles—*Metamora* and *Carabassett,* the latter by the local writer Nathaniel Deering. Meanwhile, American actors whom Neal had befriended in London were making their way on the native stage. [25] Pelby was in town during 1834; Hackett was starring in Yankee roles in New York. From there he wrote Neal on March 10, 1834, suggesting that the author turn out a brief dramatic sketch of Yankee comedy. He had in mind an afterpiece to capitalize on his own success as the frontier hero in Paulding's *The Lion of the West* and on the growing craze for Jack Downing.

The timing was right to interest Neal. He had published *The Down-Easters* just the year before. During the summer that he had been sending off the final copy to Harper, G. H. "Yankee" Hill was playing at the New Theater. There on July 22, 1833, Hill gave his first performance in Portland of Solomon Swap in *Jonathan in England.* Born George Handel Hill, son of a Boston musician, Uriah K. Hill, he had left Taunton Academy at fifteen for New York, where he got to know the actors at Chatham Garden. His friends easily led him into acting, and during the 1820s he toured New York and the southern circuit, returning to New York in 1831 as the "Yankee" lead, a part he brought to perfection. In 1833 he traveled northward from Baltimore through New York and Boston to Portland. Three years later he was to reach his greatest success in an appearance at the Drury Lane with Forrest's company. [26] In Portland, Hill was supported by Joseph S.

Jones (1809–1877) who had contributed two very popular Yankee plays to Hill's repertoire: *The People's Lawyer* (Solon Shingle) and *The Green Mountain Boy* (Jedediah Homebred). The second of these, Hill produced for his second night (July 24). After the plays, Hill told popular Yankee stories of the day. His engagement lasted through July 29. Hill was back in Portland the following summer session of 1834 when in mid-July he stirred local interest with his performance of W. R. Blake's dramatization of *Major Jack Downing at Home and Abroad.* Here "on the soil so close to Downingville," as a reviewer put it, Hill's performance could not escape the attention of a Neal pondering the Hackett proposal.[27]

But John Neal wrote to suit himself; he followed none of these box-office successes. He envisioned instead a full three-act play combining sentiment and local traits, to set forth the genuine Down-Easterner. The resulting play of *Our Ephraim,* which was ready by 1835, gave too much dignity to comic types, called for male and female Yankees in numbers beyond the resources of the current stock companies, and shifted scenes without regard to exegencies of production. Hackett could not use a "play" that read little differently from Neal's dialogue in his recent novels. Rejected by both Hackett and Hill, the manuscript survives as a result of the Yankee frugality of the author. Filling in as editor of *The New-England Galaxy,* Neal ran the rejected play in several issues.[28]

The plot is laid in the spring of 1814, approximately the time of the action in *The Down-Easters* to which it is related. Drawing on his own shopkeeping experience with counterfeit bills,[29] Neal presents a sophisticated Yankee hero who has traveled in England and Europe. Working for the governor, he acts as a secret agent in joining a group of counterfeiters who threaten the economy of the young republic. The gang is led by an Englishman whose web of intrigue against Ephraim brings him to court accused of robbery. In a dramatic courtroom confrontation of the sort Neal handles well, Yankee honesty and wits prevail over the citified cunning of the Englishman. Vindicated, Ephraim is reunited with his Quaker sweetheart, whose faith in him—though sorely tested—has remained staunch. In between, the scenes have included a quilting bee, a social supper, and militia activities. The Yankee talk is authentic, providing an excellent source of information regarding Maine dialect, circa 1830, information that has not yet been mined because of the obscure publication of the play.

Neal's cast of Yankees lard their speech with dialect words, pro-

nunciations, and idioms. The latter give a good indication of the
rhythm of Down-East talk which may still be heard in rural areas of
Maine at the present time. Among the expressions are "[she's] never
been more 'n half baked"; "there 't goes *right slap into* the woods";
"Shet your clam, will ye!"; "Cut out with a cross-cut saw, an whittled
into shape with a broad-axe, or a barn-shovel—never *know'd* which";
"as nice a little critter as ever eet beans"; "one or *tother on* em is
always etarnally out of kilker!"; "plenty to eat, *sech as tis!* An good
enough too, *what there is on't"; "Hadn't ought-a-*left it here"; "Stiff as
a mitten!—swallered a crow-bar!"; "[he's] *of a piece with* his father";
"If he ain't, I wish I may be cut up into fish-an-potatoes, and have my
hide slyvered inter razor straps, an sent to King George—same as
they did with Tecumseh's"; "puttin' things *to rights"; "*Not much the
wuss for wear tho' "; "[the love-sick Liddy] takes on dreadferly
sometimes [and is] limsey as a rag"; "[a boy courting a man's daughter
is advised] to be smellin' round somewhere else"; "I'll be swamped if
tain't"; "What you gut to say for yourself!"; "Not knowin', can't say";
"Wal! they *do say* you was *to* housekeepin there!"; "a leetle too cute
for themselves"; "I'm eenamost afeard to go. . . ."
    As indicated by the items to which italics have been added,
idiomatic use of prepositions as well as local words and colloquial
contractions are accurately captured by Neal, whose ear for variations
of speech was excellent. Exclamations from the modern-sounding
"Man alive!" to female oaths of "Dear Suzz!" and "Hytee-titee" occur
in the text. Archaic verb forms that linger in the dialect are recorded:
"no wonder she couldn't *set* still"; "she ain't *sot* still a minuit"; "just
hove himself back in the cheer [chair]"; "Guess you'll have to stay
where you *be.* . . ." Other unusual verbs include "axed" for asked,
"colloquin' " for talking, to "fodder" for to feed, "streak it" for take off
running, and "trámpoosin' " as alternative to traipsing. Yankee use of
"mistrust" is caught, as in "Not that I mistrust you now . . . but."
    Colorful dialect modifiers are sprinkled heavily in the speeches:
"*Beattermost* critter ever I see in trowzes"; "Don't be *fractious!*";
"You're a good for nothin', stingy, *meachin'* old hypocrite"; "You're a
leetle *miffed*"; "*pesky* sight warmer"; "you'll find yourself *plaguily*
mistaken"; "how've you ben?—look putty *rugged.* [Reply] I'm putty
smart Oh, I'm *cleverly*"; "he's *ryled*"; "used to be putty *slick* at
division. . . ." Also an occasional word accentuates the region: "I'm
in a most almighty *feeze,* an' can't stop"; "Esther Bray's a *gump,* an'
you're another"; "I got the *roomatiz*—all over." Clearly a failure as a
play, *Our Ephraim* is Neal's fullest detailing of Yankee dialect. From

early recording in *Seventy-Six* through *Randolph, Brother Jonathan,* and *Rachel Dyer* to the *Down-Easters* and *Our Ephraim,* he developed Yankee speech as part of his effort to "talk on paper." In the play, he lets Yankeeism run riot to the despair of the actor but the delight of the philologist.

This accurate portrayal of Maine dialect assures Neal a place among students of the American language. His experiments with a more vernacular style of writing not only paved the way for such later masters as Twain, but let him achieve an early realistic dialogue that compares favorably with the stilted conversations of Cooper's characters. It was at the time of these linguistic accomplishments that a young journalist wrote of John Neal as

a man in the east, a genuine yankee; in that land fertile in oddities, notions, plans and projects. . . . Were I called upon to portray New-England in miniature, and to speak in a single person the character of a race, with all their faults and virtues, peculiar every where, daring and confident in every thing, ready and skilful. . . . I know not how I could do it better than in the sketch . . . of *a man of the east.* [31]

That man is indeed John Neal, Down-East Yankee for better and worse.

V *Storytelling*

In the same period, beginning in 1828, Neal was turning out a substantial body of tales and short narratives—about one a year through 1846. In the 1830s he was competing for space with Hawthorne[32] in *The Token,* although always restive under the heavy editorial hand of Samuel Goodrich and breaking with him in 1836 over bowdlerization of "The Young Phrenologist."[33] Nearly one half of Neal's short narratives had a Down-East setting that relates them closely to his novels and play of the period before 1835. Until recently these contributions of Neal to the genre of the developing short story have been overlooked. But in 1962 Hans-Joachim Lang reprinted in Germany "David Whicher" and "Otter-Bag." The identification of the first of these as by Neal is discussed by Lang and Benjamin Lease,[34] and Lease devotes a chapter of his book-length study of Neal to the stories, finding the best of them "characterized by a spontaneity and exuberance conspicuously absent in Irving's graceful and witty elaborations, in Poe's masterfully controlled contributions, in Hawthorne's delicately shaded profundities."[35] These new assessments may yet restore Neal to something like the repute he had before 1840; in those days in England Mary Russell Mitford would reprint "Otter-Bag" as the first item in a three-volume collection of *Stories of American Life* (1830). And Neal, examining the developing genre, would claim for storytelling the highest purposes of giving to great men their reputations and to the upward striving of mankind the very foundations of inspiration.[36]

Noteworthy among the tales[37] with a New England setting are "Otter-Bag" and "David Whicher" (which appeared in *The Token* for 1829 and 1832 respectively), and "The Squatter" (which appeared in *The New-England Magazine* for 1835). In the first of these, Otter-Bag is an Indian serving the Revolutionary cause on the frontier. In spite of loyalty and bravery which often save the American troops, he is subjected to the distrust and open enmity of Indian haters in the army. The tale is actually a reworking of an episode excised from *Brother Jonathan* and now presented as a narrative of an old soldier of the Revolution—a device first used by Neal in *Seventy-Six*. The device effectively creates a double tone of tragicomedy. Otter-Bag's death at the hands of the very troops for whom he has scouted reveals something of the tragedy of his race, yet the garrulous presentation of the narrator—interrupted at crucial moments by the drinks that are passing around his audience—punctures the tragedy and leaves an effect of social comedy, an effect not far distant, one suspects, from the prevailing attitude toward the Indian in Neal's America. The narrative ends with the auditors' fleeing any further long-winded reminiscences of the veteran, but the tale has been told and sympathy for the Indian is all the more powerful for the cavalier attitudes of those who flee a probable retelling.

Closely related to this story is "David Whicher" which raises a folktale of a frontier encounter with Indians to a high literary level. Neal once again utilizes a somewhat ludicrous narrator to distance the brutal realities of the Maine frontier within a comic framework. A little bespectacled man who is hardly taken seriously narrates another episode of the "vanishing tribes." In the story, a deeply religious man committed to nonviolence ignores the warnings of his neighbors and travels the woods unarmed, trusting only in Providence. He is splitting a log with wedges when surprised by four savages who carry fresh scalps he recognizes as those of his children. His inner struggle between a Christian belief in the brotherhood of man and the rising human urge for vengeance is better realized by Neal than by Richard Montgomery Bird in his book-length portrayal of the Quaker scourge of the Indian in *Nick of the Woods* (1837). Bird's Nathan Slaughter is presented externally: the massacre of his family creates the Indian hater forthwith. But Neal's David Whicher does not waver in his faith even as he fights against the violence he finds in himself. He tricks the Indians into holding the riven log apart as he demonstrates the use of a wedge. Acting as God's agent he strikes the blow that knocks out the wedge and traps the four Indians by their fingers when the log springs closed upon them. Even then Whicher suffers their taunts for his failure to kill them. He departs, leaving them to whatever fate their gods reserve to them. In a return to the comic folklore material, the story brings Whicher back to the scene a year later where he sees four skeletons "still striving to tear the tree asunder"—an example, the narrator concludes, of "what the North American savage is capable of."

In "The Squatter" (1835), Neal again makes use of the harshness of the frontier to probe the psychology of character. A leisurely start to the story presents the horror and speed of forest fires in Maine, gradually leading back to the great fires of 1824 when the story proper takes place. Neal has lent reality to that story by this seemingly digressive approach. The central figure Hayes now tells his own story against a factual background. Interested in surveying a military road for defense in the North-East boundary dispute with Canada, Hayes has taken his only son with him to the deep woods. Incompatibility with his wife has caused him to leave her at home: "Had she been more of a woman and less of an angel . . ." she would have suited him better. Some time later he determines, however, on a reconciliation, leaves the boy at the camp when he returns to civilization to bring his wife back, but returns to find that fire has killed the boy. The wife goes mad, and the narrator Hayes lives on as a solitary frontiersman with a story to tell. Against the sublime horror of an unchecked forest fire, Neal allows his narrator to reveal the self-destructive powers within himself that have destroyed his family.

Similar probing of psychological depths mark "The Haunted Man" (1832) and "Idiosyncrasies" (1843). In the first of these, not only is the central character haunted by an absurd psychic hydrophobia but the narrator himself becomes haunted by the strange man. In curing him of his psychic ills, the narrator makes Neal a forerunner in the use of psychotherapy as a theme of fiction. The haunting relationship of narrator and a man with a story to tell is a repeated theme in Neal, who uses it as the frame of "Bill Frazier—The Fur-Trader" as well as in *Authorship*. The second of these psychological tales, "Idiosyncrasies," touches on autobiographical depths of fatherly tyranny and husbandly loving hate. The story illustrates the nearly self-destructive element of the perverse in a strong-willed man not unlike the author.

More humorously and with a lighter touch, the story "Courtship" (1829) relates an old bachelor's lifelong pursuit of a good wife, one that he could court off-guard and not in her "holiday-humour," preferably a young girl whom he could approach through her parents and marry to educate her in his own way. Here something of Neal's recent marriage to his young cousin provides an undercurrent to the surface of satire against the bachelor's pompous foolishness. Satire against other human and social foibles pervades "The Utilitarian" (1830), "The Young Phrenologist" (1836), and "Animal Magnetism" (1839), and against political office seeking, in "The Ins and the Outs" (1841). These stories are, however, at their best not when Neal is presenting satire but when touching on New England scenery and character. Thus "Animal Magnetism" is memorable for its opening paragraphs that delineate the Crawford Notch of the White Mountains.

When he moved still further from his natural material, his success fell off sharply. Thus his more ambitious excursions into literary tales are least successful of all. His "Will the Wizard" (1835) is a punning and superficial re-creation of the boyhood of Shakespeare dreaming in his father's shop. "The Unchangeable Jew" is an undistinguished Irvingesque tale on the then popular Wandering Jew motif, laid in medieval Spain. With these Neal was out of his element. Yet when he treated his beloved New England setting, the result was often a fine story that probed the peculiarities of character. For such tales he was once well known, so much so that an anonymous story of Yankee customs—*John Beadle's Sleigh Ride, Courtship and Marriage* (1841)—was quickly attributed to him even as it was reprinted far and wide. Neal himself clears up the mystery of authorship by assigning it to a Captain M'Clintock who was stationed at Fort Preble in Portland. (To Neal's disgust his protegé, James Brooks, who was trying to break into the journalistic scene of New York, gave himself out as the author of the popular piece; speaking bluntly against Brooks' dishonesty Neal strained their relationship as he so often did with his own zeal for honesty).

It is in his use of Yankee legends for first person narrative, then, that Neal deserves a place in the history of the American short story, a larger place than he has traditionally been afforded. His better stories are superior to the work of James Hall, whose *Legends of the West* (1832) is more often cited. Neal's lack of sentimentality, his fine control of actual speech, and his achievement of an effective tone mark his best stories as significant contributions to a native literature. They await collection and republication.

CHAPTER 6

Embattled Reformer

THE ferment of reform that swept the young nation in the 1840s was not a new thing to John Neal who had always been among the first to tilt at windmills or appoint himself champion of the underdog. As a Yankee in the Southern town of Baltimore he had argued against the *code duello* to the point of being posted as a coward. While Neal was slower to embrace the causes of temperance and abolition, under the influence of reading Godwin he early became an advocate of women's rights, and proclaimed that women were the half of the nation living a life little better than that of slaves. In a Delphian Club debate on slavery in 1823, Neal extended the scope of the topic by arguing that "the apprentice, child or wife" is no better off than the black slave. He was then thirty years old.[1]

I *Women's Rights and Wrongs*

That John Neal's espousal of the rights of women was no temporary or bandwagon joining of a reform movement is clearly seen by his speeches and writing, early and late. Through his speeches and writing Neal was devoted to the cause of women's rights from 1823 to just a few years before his death. Although the ear of prejudice was often turned deafly to his oratory and rhetoric, the force of his personality and the projection of his deep conviction had their effects. As one who thrived on controversy, opposition made him but strive the harder; as a birthright Quaker—albeit a backslider—his conscience was dedicated to any social injustice, especially that of women.

From Baltimore he carried his ideas concerning women's equality into the Bentham circle. With the young John Stuart Mill, Neal was among those who prepared topics for the London Debating Society. Neal contributed such resolutions as "That the intellectual powers of the two sexes are equal" and "That slavery *may be* justifiable." At this stage, less concerned with suffrage than with full equality, Neal argued, in a *Blackwood's* article that appears to arise from the debates, that "women are not *inferior* to men, but only unlike men, in their intellectual properties." With infectious sincerity, he makes his demand: ". . . I would have women treated like men of common sense" and concludes "Wait until women are educated like men—treated like men—and permitted to talk freely, without being put to shame, because they are women. . . ." As a consequence of this position, Neal was invited to spend a highly pleasant evening in the company of Joanna Baillie, whose plays and poems Neal greatly admired.

Back in Portland—with the intellectual example of his schoolteaching mother and sister before him—he continued the battle in the pages of *The Yankee*, particularly stressing the innate capacities of women which society failed to develop as well as thundering against the legal restraints that gave women a second-class citizenship. In these years he was training himself to the lecture platform, and soon would be supplementing his income by going on the lecture circuit. In Portland, in 1833, he tested his oratorical power when the scheduled speaker failed to show for the July 4 oration. Almost impromptu, Neal addressed the large crowd in the central and prestigious Second Parish Church on the subject of freedom. Inevitably, Neal spoke against slavery, not just the Negro's but woman's. He lashed out against English common law—still the law for most of the states—for its exclusion of the wife from holding and disposing of her property. Further, he pointed out that the woman is taxed but not allowed to vote—taxation without representation, the very abuse for which the Revolution had been fought. With both surprise and attention, the audience listened to the unexpected direction Neal took, but the final reception was that of male condescension, refusing to accept that anyone could be fully serious in presenting such views. The *Evening Advertiser* reported "This subject was discussed in a very amusing and original manner, but we suspect the fair are well satisfied with their present influence. . . ."[2] This complacent view was to haunt the early years of the movement.

The thrust of Neal's remarks is fairly typical of the period of feminism that preceded the convention of 1848 when the women's rights movement under Elizabeth Stanton and Lucretia Mott became more centrally concerned with suffrage. Neal favored the vote, but did not feel that this alone would create the sweeping changes he desired; he wanted a broadly based equality—social, educational, legal, and political. Doubtless his early reading of Godwin had led him to Mary Woolstonecraft's *Vindication of the Rights of Women*, just as his own lack of prejudice had brought him into a circle of friendship with women writers of his day. In Portland he discovered and promoted the writing careers of Ann Stephens and Elizabeth Oakes Smith, the latter of whom reports on his Tabernacle address. To Mrs. Smith he wrote about their mutual friend Margaret Fuller with witty appreciation of Fuller's fiery spirit: "Remember me to her, I pray you—as to a she-gladiator. . . ."[3] On her side, Margaret Fuller had been drawn to Neal's personality when they met in Providence in 1838, so much so that she let down her coils of hair and let him "read" the phrenological bumps of her head, twitting him on his return to Portland where as the "great man of a little town" he could relax except for "Attending Portland sidewalks, chastising inhuman teamsters, prosecuting the study of Phrenology, Magnetism. . . ." Later she had him address her school; he spoke to the girls on the vocation of women in America, and to the boys on political duties. Recalling "his magnetic genius and independent character," Margaret Fuller reports that "He gave, truly, a *manly* view, though not the view of common men, and it was pleasing to watch his countenance, where energy is animated by genius." That evening Neal and Margaret discussed woman, the Whigs, modern poetry, and Shakespeare, but she felt that "Mr. Neal does not argue quite fairly, for he uses reason while it lasts, and then helps himself out with wit, sentiment and assertion . . . but his lion-heart, and keen sense of the ludicrous, alike in himself as in others, redeem him."[4]

She was aware, then, of Neal's work on behalf of women when she came to strike her own blow in *The Dial* in 1843 and in the expanded form of *Woman in the Nineteenth Century* (1845); for both of them were far ahead of popular sentiment. It was not until 1848 that trending-setting New York State passed the Property Bill that gave women control over their own property.

Likewise Mrs. Smith in her own formative years had responded to Neal's oratory, recalling later, "I went to hear him speak in the City Hall, which was densely crowded. He used no notes and spoke with great force and originality for nearly two hours. His manly bearing, readiness, and vivacity fired my enthusiasm. What he said of women responded to what had been so long fermenting in my own mind that I was deeply affected."[5] She also witnessed at least one of his appearances in New York City on behalf of women's rights.

II   *Women's Rights in New York City*

Neal's opportunity for a larger impact came in 1843. He was editing *Brother Jonathan,* an inexpensive New York weekly. Under the auspices of the Mechanics' Library Association—before the Portland branch of which Neal had often lectured—a series of topics were being presented to the public at the Broadway Tabernacle, a rotundaed structure seating several thousand. On January 24, Neal spoke on "Rights of Women" before a packed house, for, reported the New York *Herald* on the following day, "the ladies seemed determined to muster all their forces for the occasion. Even John Neal seemed somewhat discomforted when he rose in the full blaze of that fascination and becoming beauty." It is doubtful that the speaker was long discomforted as he eloquently leveled his charges against the slavery of women. To his usual points he added that the original Declaration of Rights of 1774 had spoken of the rights of the *inhabitants.* Were not women inhabitants? Were not women persons to also enjoy the protected rights of the nation? Then addressing his challenge to the men, Neal argued that it was men who had usurped all power to themselves, ". . . Men have obtained mastery over Women, not by superior virtue, nor by superior understanding, but by the original accident of superior strength. . . ." His earnestness, however, met with little sympathy from a conservative audience, which was determined to find him entertaining and nothing more. In a refusal to take seriously his message, the *Tribune* editorialized with confessed "inveterate masculine prejudice" that the subject was too absurd even to argue.

Stimulated rather than discouraged by the attitude of the press, Neal returned to the Tabernacle the following week, turning his announced topic of "General Reading" into an answer to the reviews, which had indeed been his recent reading. The *Herald* spoke cruelly of this second performance as the "jokes of a man fond of humor and fantastic notions." But within the month, Neal was back. Undaunted, he agreed to debate on February 8 two editors, Park Benjamin of the rival *New World,* [6] and Colonel William Leete Stone of the *Commercial Advertiser.* Neal later complained that his opponents monopolized the time and gave him no chance for rebuttal. But he did have his supporters; Mrs. Elizabeth Oakes Smith recalled the occasion in her *Autobiography:*

The audience was not a large one, but was of the highest quality in culture and refinement; and being in a great degree composed of intellectual persons of old and esteemed families, was naturally a conservative one. Some enthusiasm was manifested at the fine manly appearance of John Neal, his superior address and thoroughly gentlemanly breeding no less than for the exhibition of original thought and outbursts of eloquence.

But she also remembered to report the more general impression of Neal's blow struck on behalf of women:

Mr. Charles F. Hoffman was one of Neal's auditors and listened to him with great interest. To a thoroughly conservative mind like Hoffman's, his views seemed not only ultra but dangerous.

"What do you think of Mr. Neal?" I asked at the close of the discourse.

"I think him an enthusiast, but a right manly man, and thoroughly the gentleman."

"But I meant to ask what do you think of his opinions?"

"I think they would take woman from her throne where she is worshiped, to place her in the furrows to be bespattered."[7]

Women were to be left on their throne, and right-minded women were assumed to be content to exert mere moral influence from their enshrined height; such was the popular myth of the day.

Neal was far from ready to retire from the battle. In June, he published his original, controversial Tabernacle address in *Brother Jonathan.* Following numbers carried on a newspaper debate between Neal as editor and Mrs. Eliza W. Farnham, who argued against political equality since woman had her own distinct sphere of action and she need only exert the moral influence of her sex to right her wrongs. She was supported in her views by Horace Greeley who the night before the Tabernacle debate had editorialized: "It is not necessary to the redress of these grievances that our women shoulder muskets or cast ballots. All that is required is simply that they know their wrongs and firmly, mildly petition for their redress. Let them do this and the evils from which they suffer will vanish forever." Neal knew better, and so he argued with Mrs. Farnham firmly yet mildly. With final politeness Mrs. Farnham cut off the debate by begging a woman's right to the last word.[8] As a gentleman, Neal yielded, saving his eventual last word for a later time.

In their exchange of opinions, Neal had quoted Mrs. Farnham: "But woman's declaration of rights, you say, is 'I am a wife and a mother! To be these is my *freedom,* to be other is slavery.' But suppose she happened to be neither,—according to your own definition, she is a *slave.* We have hundreds of thousands of women in this

country who are neither wives nor mothers—nor ever will be—
would you leave them nothing to console them?"[9] Neal's own twin
sister was among the hundreds of thousands who being neither wife
nor mother were to devote life to one of the few careers open to
women—schoolteaching. When he came to write *True Womanhood*
in 1859, he perhaps had Rachel Neal in mind, as he had had in making
his unmarried heroine of *Rachel Dyer* a namesake. At least the novel
is in large part an answer to the Mrs. Farnhams who were content to
relegate woman to the roles of wife and mother only.

III   *True Womanhood*

For some years in the 1850s, friends including Longfellow had
been urging Neal to write a new novel. His early experiments with
fiction lay forty years in the past; could he sustain a novel for the more
sophisticated readers now? At the close of the decade he complied
with these urgings with *True Womanhood*, the publication of which
by Ticknor and Fields of Boston Longfellow helped arrange.

While the plot is still a farago of mysteries of the gothic sort—a
poison ring with a strange Oriental background, a mysterious Quaker
in eighteenth century garb of knee pants, an ambiguously good-bad
brother—the novel also contains some of Neal's best writing. The
story is presented with heavy dependence on dialogue, handled with
Neal's mature absence of "he saids." But, as so often, he overdoes
even a good thing. The near absence of description and narration
through long tracts of the book allows the dialogue to sink too often
into dullness. Yet, the opening chapter paints a good picture of
contemporary New York society. Reflecting contemporary events,
Neal traces the rapid rise of crime following the financial panic of
1857–1858; with the accompanying inability of the police to cope with
robberies and muggings. A troubled public turns toward reform and
religion. Not without a hint of satire for the sudden shifts of city fads,
Neal chronicles the religious revival that is at least partly the social
thing to do. In general, however, Neal, who had himself returned to
formal religion in his time of personal trouble over his son's death, is
serious about the revivals he presents; in 1851, he, his wife, and his
sister had joined the Congregational Church.

Again good social history is set forth in chapters dealing with the
"business-men's prayer meetings" at the Episcopal Church on
Broadway after an evangelical spirit has been stimulated among the
worried businessmen by the examples set by the ladies. Thus, Neal's
heroine Julia is devoutly religious, but also independent and

strong-minded. She emerges from the twists and turns of a romantic plot as Neal's exemplar of "true womanhood," an answer to his former critics like Mrs. Farnham.

In one of the two well-realized trial scenes, Julia is at first modestly terrified in the witness box, but under the badgering of a belligerent cross-examination,

> She felt that she was no longer a witness, but a wronged woman, with nobody at hand to take her part, and that, while treated with a great appearance of respect and courtesy, the gentleman was trying to show himself off, at her expense; and the blood flashed through her veins like fire, as she answered very slowly, but with a musical vibration. . . . In a word, *her woman's rights being outraged* and her sex, in her, she determined to vindicate herself.[10]

Besides concern for her uncle at whose trial she is testifying, Julia is properly concerned about a wayward cousin Arthur, yet the reader is allowed to sympathize with his flight from a mother and sister who are smothering his high spirits in an attempt to make him "more serious." Another young man of the family has long disappeared, having informed Julia before his departure that he was going "where I shall not be checked, and watched, and thwarted, and waylaid at every turn, by my best friends" (*I*, 57). Arthur has stayed, rebelling into epicureanism that his family rightfully finds dangerous. He seems almost an early Pater when he expresses his philosophy:

> To linger over a new book . . . as I do over this, and be unwilling to come to an end, as a cat would play with a mouse, toying with the fruitage that hangs in our way, dallying with what we most love, and tasting and forbearing; these are to me the highest evidence of a true flavor, and a right appreciation. (*I*, 103)

The climax to the several plots comes in a second trial scene. Uncle George stands accused of business fraud, and appearances are against him. His defense attorney, Mr. Fay, is felt to be too glib and hence insincere. But all comes right. Fay is in command of the courtroom with all the drama of a proto-Perry Mason. At the end of the first day of trial, the tide is turning toward Uncle George. It only takes the last-minute arrival of the long-lost nephew Charles as a surprise witness, bearing new documents that clear the accused and return him to prosperity. The prodigal has returned and returned reformed, for he has found God in South America and can now win the hand of saintly Edith.

But no such traditionally romantic fate awaits Mr. Fay. He woos the sprightly Julia. She answers both Fay and Mrs. Farnham: ". . . I do not believe that marriage is a condition absolutely indispensable for the happiness of woman, or for the development of true woman-hood; . . . I would rather live, and rather die, in such single blessed-ness as I have sometimes heard of . . ." (*I*, 462). For all his lawyerlike qualities, Fay has failed because, Julia goes on to point out, his religious views are too different from her own. She speaks for an alternate life-style, but must pass one final temptation to accept the social norm. When her true love, the erring Arthur, reforms and confesses his own love for her, she also refuses his offer of marriage because he is her first cousin. With this second renunciation of the roles of wife and mother, Julia emerges as the unmarried heroine who lives happily ever after, single yet with true womanhood.[11]

While Neal's major contribution to women's rights came in the early years—before the Property Bill of 1848—he neither forgot the battle in the later period nor was he forgotten by the suffragettes. Mrs. Smith read a long letter by Neal before the Woman's Rights Convention of 1852 in Syracuse, New York. As late as 1869 he was contributing heavily to the militant *The Revolution* of New York, correcting "Horace Greeley and his 'Notions of Woman's Rights' " as well as attacking "Our Disinterred Ante-Diluvians." Even after his death, Neal was remembered in the History of Woman Suffrage by Elizabeth C. Stanton, Susan B. Anthony, and Matilda J. Gage.[12]

IV   *Other Reform Issues*

The cause of women was by far not the only cause into which Neal poured his seemingly endless energies. He opposed duelling both by speech and writing, especially in the pages of his first novel *Keep Cool*. He opposed lotteries for robbing the poor (see *Logan*). He opposed both imprisonment for debt and the still controversial death penalty, "having no belief in the wisdom of strangulation, for men, women, and children, however much they might seem to deserve it, and being fully persuaded that the worst men have the most need of repentance, and that they who are unfit to live, are still more unfit to die."[13]

Smaller reforms, too, concerned him. As a republican, he opposed all use of titles and never missed a chance to satirize the habit of lawyers signing themselves "esquire." As the son and brother of teachers, he was often involved in educational reform, singling out grammar books as particular offenders, more often hindering the development of good writing than promoting it. In health reform he was a distant relative and close friend of Mary Gove who sought to cure cases of nerves with good water and fulfilled love; he met with sympathy Dr. Sylvester Graham when Emerson's "poet of bran bread and pumpkins" spread his gospel of health through diet and exercise on a speaking tour of Maine in 1833.

Already convinced of the value of exercise, Neal had established, soon after his return from England, a gymnasium for the young men of Portland in the old town hall, later moving it to Munjoy Hill. Here he worked them on parallel bars and over an early obstacle course of ditches for leaping. In addition to the manly arts of boxing and fencing, he helped introduce gymnastics to the country, for he had in London conditioned himself under the rough regimen of Carl Voelker. His years in Baltimore and London—spent driving himself to succeed at law and literature by frenzied study and writing—had led to two attacks of fainting. Frightened that even his robust health had been overabused, he set himself a schedule of health that soon included boxing, fencing, and workouts in Voelker's new gymnasium. Utterly converted to Swedish gymnastics, he carried his efforts to establish gymnastics in America beyond Portland, urging Jefferson to make a gymnastic school part of the University of Virginia. In the newly established *American Journal of Education* (Boston),[14] he reached a larger audience by articles on Voelker's gymnasium, on exercises, and on outstanding teachers of gymnastics. This was in 1826, with a final exhortation the following year for America to develop gymnastics schools on the line of British institutions and his own school in Portland. In 1828 he was invited to establish a gymnasium at Bowdoin College.

At about the same time Neal was invited by the Temperance Association in Portland to deliver its annual address [15] at the First Parish Church where its pastor, the scholarly Dr. Nichols, had spoken just the year before. According to Neal (*WR*, 355) he never before had held the large lecture platform, but he set to work to meet the engagement as still another challenge. He did not yet realize it, but the occasion heralded the beginning of his frequent appearances as a strong and popular lecturer; Neal was later to supplement his income by following the lyceum circuit, where he spoke on such varied topics as "literature, eloquence, the fine arts, political economy, temperance, poets and poetry, public-speaking, our pilgrim fathers, colonization, law and lawyers, the study of languages, natural-history, phrenology, women's-rights, self-education, self-reliance, and self-distrust" (*WR*, 353).

On this first appearance, he was well received by a large audience who heard the usual arguments against the evils of drink. But a typical Neal touch was added when he called for a fifty year revolution against addiction to liquor—which would be a greater cause and greater struggle than the American Revolution just fifty years past. Temperance in this early period of the movement still meant temperance not abstention; it was temperance that Neal espoused, although his cousin Neal Dow would soon be whipping up sentiment for the total banning of all spirits.

Some years later in 1836 he would again address the Portland group as it was about to add wine to the list of proscribed drinks. Stalling for time by moving adjournment of the meeting he returned to present a well-reasoned and well-documented case for moderate use of wine. Although he himself was abstemious, it was well known that Neal had in his new home a wine cellar stocked with some five or six hundred bottles of madeira, port, sherry, and muscat. He was politely—on this occasion—if coldly received; but he did prevail for the time being.[16] Only three years later, however, the association voted to add wine to the prohibited list. In 1846 the Neal Dow party prevailed and Maine went dry, the first state to pass prohibition legislation. Typically Neal had argued not merely for wine, but for the "moderate use of pure wine," taking the moment to attack adulterations. In his old age, recalling these days, he mused, "What I wanted was a *pure* wine, and that, I then believed, and still believe would promote the cause of temperance. . . . But where shall we go for pure wine? Not on earth, I'm afraid, nor anywhere. . . ." (*WR*, 367)

Regarding drink, Neal was his own man. He would enlist in the cause of sane temperance but was unwilling to join the increasing tide of fanaticism. Such independence is often misunderstood and so was John Neal. Increasing bitterness grew between him and his cousin—perhaps they were too much alike and ill shared the public spotlight. Quarrels over family inheritance deepened the enmity. Meantime tragedy was developing in Neal's immediate family. His son James had become addicted to drink. In 1851 he was sent to Pierpont to see if the minister-friend's influence could keep him to his pledge, but the problem was beyond anyone's control. Neal Dow cruelly used the son to strike the father. In a thinly veiled article identifying Neal by his well-known mansion, Dow referred to the "skeleton in that house," the son who had been ruined by a father's introducing him to drink by serving wine at dinner. Four years later the unhappy James was dead of fever in the ranks of General Walker's fillibustering army of Nicaragua.[17] The bereaved father could never forgive nor forget the unwarranted attack by Dow. In his autobiography, Neal devotes the entire twentieth chapter to a rehearsal of his own endeavors in the temperance cause, painfully returning to the Dow attack, reprinting the charge, and refuting it.

Neal's own confessional account of how as a boy he tried liquor, dipped sugar into brandy, went on to rum punch, and then gave them all over when he found a habit forming is paralleled in his story "Robert Steele" which he used to fill out the second volume of *The Down-Easters* in 1833. While the story has some local details of dialect and folkways of "Yarmouth" and so can be partially justified as rounding out the portraits of the novel to which it is appended, the central plot has no connection with the novel, for it is a mere thread on which to hang the episodes of a temperance tract. Robert Steele is first presented in a drunken rage in which he gravely wounds an officer. The narrator then learns the story of Steele's life from the doctor who is his stepfather:

When Robert Steele was a boy, he got fond of strong drink, no matter why, no matter how—first he loved to dip sugar into sweet wine and eat the sugar; then he dipped into stronger and yet stronger wine—after a while, he tried brandy-and-water—then a little more brandy and a little less sugar; 'till he drank as you do now, a glass of brandy-and-water every day before dinner (DE 2. 199).

In the opinion of the doctor, only a serious shock can now effect a reform from the grip of alcohol: he arranges to keep secret from Steele the fact that the officer has not died, nor has Steele's wife who was left in a faint when the drunkard was taken off to jail. Facing utter ruin, Steele reforms, is released, and ". . . is now a reformed man—a good husband—a good father—a good friend. The fright saved him."

Thus concludes Neal's temperance story. In this and his addresses, Neal's position on temperance reform was a matter of public knowledge, so that Neal Dow's attack had been especially hurtful and unjust. But it was John Neal's fate to be ever a storm center. His individual mind did not often lead him to popular opinion. As the temper of the times became more and more polarized, he remained a spokesman for a middle ground, opposing the extremity of a state law that forbade all spirits. But his middle road on temperance was as little a highway to popularity as was his extreme view on women's rights.

Likewise unpopular was his stand on the question of abolition on slavery. More than most New Englanders, Neal was aware, from his Baltimore years, of the magnitude of the problem. Writing in *Blackwood's* in 1825, he foresaw the "probable separation of the states" over the issue of slavery, and he also foresaw no easy solution. Having grown up in a Portland which had a population of possibly two hundred Negroes,[18] he further understood that freedom did not automatically grant social equality. A revealing satire of prejudice is dramatically presented in his *Down-Easters*. On the boat from Philadelphia to Baltimore, a Yankee trader turns the conversation against Southerners who keep "a hundred or two o'great nasty bull-niggers apiece, jest to sharpen their knives on"—"I've been there, I tell ye, an' I know what I'm sayin' of. . . ." This is followed by the sexual charge of miscegenation: "Haint they sold their own flesh an' blood many a time to get money for a cock-fight or a hoss-race?" But he concludes, "What should we care, comin' from a land o' liberty where there aint no niggers to speak of." At this point the group has been joined by the Virginian Middleton who questions the Yankee in such a way as to elicit the depth of Northern social prejudice against the Negro. With keen satire, Neal allows his Yankee to unconsciously reveal himself: "do ye think we keep company with niggers, or make friends of 'em, hey?" He goes on to speak of the way in which "in our part of the country they think themselves most as good as white folks, every bit election-days." And when Middleton asks if they tax them, the Yankee responds: "Tax 'em! to be sure we do; they are free-niggers that way."

As the satire continues, the Yankee recounts the history of one Sambo Smith who was a hero in the Revolution, but is now kept in his socially inferior place. Yet, to the Yankee's ire, at elections Sambo votes his own mind. "Wunt vote for nobody't he dont like, no matter who gives a recommend. . . ." Unable to restrain himself longer, Middleton stalks away at this point and the topic shifts.[19]

As aware of Northern injustice and bigotry as he was of Southern, Neal came to a position favoring colonization rather than full abolition. He aided the formation of a Colonization Society at Portland—reported in the Boston abolition paper *The Liberator* on July 27, 1833, and in the October 24, 1835, issue a Zedekiah Downing letter is devoted to Neal. Yet sadly, the extremism of Garrison led to a quarrel and break. In part Neal was intolerant of anyone's extremes but his own. As he broke with Neal Dow, so he broke with Garrison, although a post–Civil War reconciliation did take place.[20]

In his personal dealing with Negroes, Neal is clear. The man who had been a Quaker boy in a Congregational town knew something of prejudice at first hand. Two incidents reveals Neal's unprejudiced and friendly responses.[21] The first of these occurred at the time of his arrival back in Portland from England. His enemies posted Neal as insane and in the care of "Dr. Stephen Jones, M.D., an eminent African Physician," actually a town character who was hired to follow Neal about the streets. Although the hostility of the town did little, as Neal said with uncharacteristic understatement, to "soothe my irritation, or sweeten my temper," he did nothing to "Dr. Jones," whom he saw as a harmless dupe in the cruel game. Finding Jones well paid for his part, Neal gave full consent to his following everywhere, until the joke grew cold and too expensive to its perpetrators.

The second incident is even more revealing of Neal's attitude. He attempted to integrate his new gymnasium with a class of some half-dozen young Negroes. The Portland youth already enrolled—all but two fellow Quakers—refused fully and repeatedly to allow them to use the facilities, even with Neal donating his services to the class. Again with restraint, Neal reports "This, I acknowledge, went far to dishearten me; for what was bodily training, compared with spiritual training? What a system of gymnastics, weighed against humanity and consistency?"[22] His attempt at dealing with the race problem on a personal level of educational and social development failed, and so did his interest in the gymnasium to which he had given a year of free service.

CHAPTER 7

Critic, Patron, Hack

LIKE Poe, Neal was at heart a magazinist, throwing his considerable energy and talent into the editing of various periodicals over a span of forty years.[1] His first experience had come in Baltimore where he prepared the June, 1818, issue of *The Portico*.[2] The founding editor, Dr. Tobias Watkins, who had recently been appointed assistant surgeon-general of the United States, left the preparation of what turned out to be the final issue to Neal, its major contributor during the preceeding two years. The hoppers were nearly empty and the young substitute editor filled the pages with his own reviews, including a perceptive study of "Childe Harold's Pilgrimage, Canto IV." But his uncongenial excursion into philosophy—"Man not a Free Agent"—ran twenty-seven pages, and, said Neal, "knocked it in the head."[3] *The Portico's* days were, however, already numbered with the breaking up of the original group of the Delphian Club; the demise of its journal cannot be laid to Neal's editorship. Otherwise he would not, a few months later, have been asked by Paul Allen, another of the Delphians, to fill in for him as editor of the *Federal Republican and Baltimore Telegraph*. Neal had also contributed to this journal as early as 1817. Now during February through July, 1819, he saw its issues through the press. These two experiences with editing in Baltimore were a foretaste of his launching his own ambitious *Yankee*[4] in January, 1828. It marked his reentry into the American literary scene after his years abroad and was his platform for reestablishing his reputation.

I A Yankee Circle

During the two years of its existence *The Yankee* as edited by John Neal was a stimulating vehicle for new ideas, a voice for Neal's considerable critical talents, and an outlet for previously undis-

111

covered writers. The forthrightness of the editor was reflected in every issue. It was this openness and honesty that impressed a contemporary who wrote of the weekly,

Articles, which for their boldness and audacity could find place in no other columns, were as acceptable to our unflinching editor, as the mother's milk that gave him his incipient vigor. If they were erroneous, he retracted like a true man, in the next issue. Were they true, as soon prevent the soul of John Brown from marching on, as move him to a retraction.[5]

With characteristic lack of modesty, Neal himself knew the value and uniqueness of what he was doing. In the sixth issue he advised subscribers to get covers and preserve the paper, for "Our *Yankees* are worth it. . . ."[6] As editor he labored with love for five hundred dollars a year payable in books,[7] but his true reward was in earning back his place of acceptance in his hometown. Early issues, therefore, contain a good deal of self-vindication in long articles on England that demonstrate how little he had sold out his native land. Yet he refrained from a position of unexamined anti-British sentiment, for issues in March, 1828, contain praise of Shelley, followed the next month by defenses of Leigh Hunt and Byron. Neal also hoped to introduce to America the thought of Jeremy Bentham.

His interest in Benthamism had, of course, been reinforced by his residence in the philosopher's household, and he now dedicated his weekly to spreading Bentham's ideas, at least as he understood them. But he had quarreled in England with most of the younger utilitarians, and too often his columns contain splenetic attacks on John Bowring and John Stuart Mill. Even his portraits of Bentham reveal a crotchety and eccentric old man rather than a seminal thinker. His most positive contribution to the introduction of utilitarian principles into America turns out to be in the practical field of prison reform. Drawing on the *Panopticon* of Bentham, Neal ran a six-part series on "Penitentiary Systems" during 1829. Yet, in spite of the motto blazoned on *The Yankee*—"The greatest happiness of the greatest number"—Neal's service to popularizing utilitarianism was, at last, mixed in effect. He may actually have done the philosophy harm by his own intemperate espousal; one reviewer concluded,

Bentham's views we believe, are not appreciated in this country owing to two causes—the fact that they were originally published in the French language, and the more unfortunate fact, that that versatile and unbearably egotistical genius, John Neal, undertook, from the very best motives, to introduce them to the American public.[8]

For all that Neal's Benthamism created intellectual excitement and ferment in the pages of *The Yankee*, the more lasting impact of the paper was upon the rising generation of writers, many of whom found in Neal their first sympathetic editor. Actively seeking native writers who would fulfil his dream of a truly native literature, his friendly and insightful responses were crucial to a number of struggling young hopefuls. Whittier, among them, would write to Neal in 1828: "I have just written something for your consideration. . . . If you don't like it, say so privately; and *I will quit poetry, and everything also of a literary nature,* for I am sick at heart of the business. . . ."[9] Neal responded by rushing the poem into print within the month, and later on wrote to Whittier with the good advice not to worry so much about hostile reviews.[10] In November, 1828, he was one of the few to see merit in Hawthorne's first novel *Fanshawe;* he reviewed it in encouraging terms while noting the signs of haste and inexperience. Neal was also perceptive in his reviews of Longfellow and N. P. Willis: of the poet he wrote "As for Mr. Longfellow, he has a fine genius and a pure and safe taste, and all that he wants, we believe, is a little more energy, and a little more stoutness" (January 23, 1828). He also had good words for the Boston poet J. G. Percival and Portland's own Grenville Mellen, but his early discovery of Poe was probably his most signal critical achievement.

The years of *The Yankee* were those of crisis in the life of Edgar Allan Poe: his recent break with John Allan had resulted in his enlistment in the army. A partial reconciliation, effected by Mrs. Allan in her deathbed, led Allan to help Poe gain an appointment to West Point. But by 1829 he was living on a small allowance in Baltimore with his brother and Mrs. Maria Clemm, while hoping that the new edition of his poems would be better received than had been the Boston edition of 1827. Personal crisis and professional discouragement in his hoped-for writing career had brought him to a point of low morale, when from Maine and the pen of John Neal came the first essential understanding of his poetic talent:

If E. A. P. of Baltimore—whose lines about *Heaven* [later titled "Fairyland"], though he professes to regard them as altogether superior to anything in the whole range of American poetry. . . . , are, though, nonsense, rather exquisite nonsense—would but do himself justice, [he] might

make a beautiful and perhaps a magnificent poem. There is a good deal here
to justify such a hope.

So wrote Neal in the September issue of the paper. Certainly not
unqualified praise, but just, and to the struggling Poe, sufficient to
raise his battered hopes.

Poe responded with a long letter[11] detailing his orphaned childhood and his publication plans. He seized on Neal's words regarding
the possibilities of his writing a beautiful and perhaps magnificent
poem, calling them "the very first words of encouragement I ever
remember to have heard." He was considering dedicating his new
volume of poetry to Neal, who felt that such a dedication would be of
little help to the young poet. The compromise was that "Tamerlane"
was indeed dedicated to John Neal in Poe's *Al Aaraaf, Tamerlane,
and Minor Poems* (1829). From the prepublication galleys Neal
printed selections in the last issue of *The Yankee* (December, 1829),
praising the poems, which he found to be a quality that entitle the
poet to "deserve to stand high—very high—in the estimation of the
shining brotherhood."[12]

Poe was soon to turn to the writing of tales, where he was
influenced by Neal, particularly by the latter's theory of effect.[13] As
late as 1840, Poe would recall to Neal the early encouragement he had
received in *The Yankee:* ". . . you gave me the first jog in my literary
career. . . ."[14]

Meanwhile, the stir created in Portland by the return of John Neal
as its most famous, or infamous, author was not without its effect upon
the younger writers of the area. Neal had long been friends with
Grenville Mellen, who was to break with the family tradition of law
(his father rose to be chief justice of Maine) and publish poetry and
tales in the gift books and journals. Mellen's brother Frederic, a
talented artist, was one of a group who had become acquainted with
Neal's work while they were still undergraduates at Bowdoin College. These included Nathaniel Hawthorne and Henry W. Longfellow. At the nearby Waterville College, now Colby, Seba Smith and
James Brooks were inspired by Neal to follow literary journalism.
Brooks is typical of those in the young college groups:

I was a college-boy when I first became acquainted with Mr. Neal as a writer;
and late at night I used to read his "Errata," not the best nor the worst of his
novels, with an intense and thrilling interest, and feel strange thoughts as I
was wrought upon by his wild but ungovernable imagination. He was the
hero of our circle.[15]

Neal was selected to give the address to the alumni of Colby College in 1830, and in 1836 received an honorary masters degree from Bowdoin. To this nucleus of writers, Neal drew also a number of women. Mrs. Sally Wood, novelist of the older generation, was a resident in Portland where her last volume, a collection of tales, appeared in 1827 and was reviewed favorably by Neal. The young Elizabeth Oakes, who was to marry Seba Smith, was strongly influenced by Neal, as was Ann Stephens, who in her Portland years edited *The Portland Magazine* (1836–1837) and *The Portland Sketch Book* (1836).

After 1836 many of the group scattered to Boston and New York, but Neal's first decade in Portland was filled with the stimulus of a congenial literary group. Thereafter he kept in touch by voluminous correspondence and travel, not only with the lesser known members of the circle, but with Longfellow, Whittier, Poe, N. P. Willis, and Lowell. He was also active in fostering music and painting, writing reviews, acting as patron, everywhere demanding American support for American arts. *The Yankee* was, as it were, a catalyst to the cultural strivings of the region, as struggling painters as well as writers found a patron in its editor.

II   *Art Criticism*

Just as Neal brought to his criticism of poetry and fiction his own practice in the genres, so to his criticism of American art he brought his own experience with drawing and portraiture. He always held that only a practitioner could truly understand and criticize an art form. During the interim between his leaving a clerk's job in Portland and his move to further mercantile ventures in Boston and Baltimore, he joined an itinerant teacher of penmanship. From the skill of fine handwriting was an easy step to India-ink portrait sketches and profiles which Neal sold for three dollars a sitting in the Down-East towns of Hallowell, Augusta, Waterville. Without training, he had sufficient skill of hand and eye to capture likenesses, but more importantly he developed a lifelong interest in the visual arts— especially paintings and sketches, loved for their first fine frenzy.[16]

He had grown up without the chance to view good paintings, but an innate love of art developed quickly as opportunity for observation came his way. From the time he hit Boston in 1814 he developed a lifetime habit of looking at pictures wherever he went—New York, Philadelphia, Boston, and later London and Paris. Galleries and commercial museums were beginning to open in the major American centers. Traveling exhibits of historical canvasses, for example those by Trumbull, were making their way along the coastal city route. In Baltimore, there was the chance for Neal to study painting in depth. There, Rembrandt Peale had in 1814 opened his museum. Neal moved intimately in the Peale circle, sitting for details in paintings, having his own portrait taken, and wooing Rembrandt's daughter Rosalba. From this experience came his first commentary on American artists, included as letters by the fictional hero Molton in *Randolph*.

These remarks in turn developed into essays published in *Blackwood's* during his stay in England. There he visited West's studios, lodged for a time with Thomas Sully's nephew Robert, and sat for a portrait by Chester Harding. His trip to Paris took him to the Louvre. Back in America he frequented the museums and exhibits of New York and Boston. In 1828 in *The Yankee* appear his reviews and critiques that continue into *Brother Jonathan*, the journal, and culminate in a series for the *Atlantic Monthly* in 1868–1869.[17] By then Neal had been overshadowed by the work of William Dunlap and C. Edwards Lester, who in his *The Artists of America* (1846) commended Neal's art criticism as that of "a gentleman of exquisite taste and analytical genius." This judgment is corroborated by Harold Dickson who finds that ". . . to a remarkable degree Neal's opinions, hasty, impulsive, sometimes flippantly offered though they may be, have stood the trying test of time."[18]

In keeping with his general aesthetic, Neal had a preference for unlabored effects, "an offhand, free, sketchy style, without high finish," as he called it. One sees an illustration of this preference in his first patronage of the artist Charles Codman whom he sought out on his return to Portland.

Codman (1800–1842) had come to that city around 1822 from an apprenticeship of painting clock faces for Willard of Roxbury and fire buckets for Penniman of Boston. To this mundane level of art, Codman added instruction in painting landscapes in oil.[19] In the year before Neal's return, the struggling artist had received a special commission to decorate the Elm Tavern in Portland.

Rufus Porter[20] had recently passed through the town painting scenic wall coverings at a rate considerably lower than the cost of the much desired imported French wall papers. Codman was to duplicate as "dry frescoes" the effects of French wall paper or Porter imitations. The results caught the eye of Neal in 1827.

Neal, who rather fancied his role as patron of the arts, in after years recounted several times his discovery of "one of our earliest and finest landscape painters."[21] Neal's story grew better and less modest with the years, but its essential outline remained constant. The murals themselves have long since disappeared,[22] and only Neal's description remains. Keeping close to the decorativeness of the French wallpaper they were supposed to imitate, these murals according to Neal's description cannot have been especially good, for "There were trees and houses—or rather the skeletons of both—sky and water—or the shadows of both—mere outlines, and all of a color. And yet—the hand of the master was there—no, not of the master, but the hand of a peculiar, undisciplined, unpretending *natural* genius was there."[23] As Neal passed through the room which Codman had decorated, he was struck by the "boldness and beauty of some passages," and particularly by the foliage, which, although in black and white, yet had a "wild" and natural spirit. It was the spontaneity and dash of execution that attracted Neal, because it fitted his own romantic doctrine of the arts. Hurrying to Codman's studio, the flamboyant Neal overwhelmed the artist, whose retiring modesty must have contrasted humorously with the opposite traits of his self-appointed patron. There Neal cruelly rejected as wretched an oil landscape that Codman thought his best (". . . it had been literally worked to death—tame, spiritless and feather-bedish . . ."), but before leaving he placed an order for a landscape on the condition that Codman would leave it "unfinished, rough-cast." More than this, Neal hastened about among his friends, "selling" the worth of their Portland artist. He succeeded in getting orders from Simon Greenleaf and T. A. Deblois,[24] and the three commissioned pictures when completed established Codman as "our landscape painter" with all the townspeople. Neal later claimed that "From this day, Codman kept busy, and having about given up his fire-bucket business and sign-painting . . . began to throw off marine-views, mountain scenery, and summer-landscapes . . . until there are few collections, in our city or neighborhood without a Codman."[25]

Whether Charles Codman's artistic path was straight and easy from the moment he met Neal is questionable, yet Neal must be credited with popularizing the struggling artist and giving him the first informed criticism of his work he had received. Certainly an increased artistic productivity in the years following 1827 took Codman's activities into areas outside Portland. A year after the meeting, Codman had a landscape in the second annual exhibit of the Boston

Athenaeum. Very likely Neal was responsible for this entry, for we know that he followed with interest the Athenaeum exhibits and had plans, which remained unfulfilled, for a Portland-sponsored show.[26]

Although Codman did not exhibit in the next year (1829), he was busy perfecting his style and accumulating canvases. He experimented with still life,[27] and worked out a personal technique for foliage. To simulate light and shade on individual leaves, he painstakingly worked over the damp paint with the point of a pin, a method which infuriated Neal but which achieved an effect that is still striking.[28]

Neal's discovery and stimulation of Charles Codman is typical of his efforts on behalf of artists in all media. In the field of art, there is little doubt that his patronage, his frequent reviews of exhibits, his editorial exhorting of the public to support the arts, his own commissions and collecting of painting and sketches, all helped to develop the growing market for both landscapes and portraits that were to fill the parlor walls of nineteenth century America. He himself was a factor in making real his nationalistic boast of May 1835 that, taking "the whole body of our portrait painters together, we have produced more good ones, and perhaps I might go so far as to say, more excellent ones, within the same period, than any other people upon the earth of three times our number and wealth."[29] Once again Neal had scored a first, for his remarks in *Randolph* (1823) appear to be the earliest American art criticism.[30]

III *Hackwork and Retrospection*

By the 1840s, the Portland circle had dispersed and Neal—in increasing literary isolation—was involved in business affairs and family responsibilities. His writing was sporadic. The sorrows of human existence were touching him deeply: His daughter Eleanor died, just under two years of age, in 1847. Two years later his mother also died. He was further troubled by the drinking problem of his eldest son James. Turning to religion, Neal joined the traditional Congregational Church in 1851, together with his twin sister Rachel and his wife—all of them converts from Quakerism, although he had long been out of the Society. This religious experience found outlet in his statement of creed, *One Word More*, published in Portland and Boston in 1854. Two years later tragedy struck again when James died in Nicaragua, aged twenty-five. The death of his Aunt Rachel, Neal's only sister, followed less than two years later. As family sorrows occupied Neal, little came of his various literary projects. He had planned a two-volume history of American literature as early as 1850, but did not proceed with it. So few were his publications at this time that Hawthorne in 1845 could speculate that Neal "surely has long been dead, else he never could keep himself so quiet."[31]

Yet energy remained. In 1858 he made a trip to Cairo, Illinois, to see at first hand the town development in which he was a shareholder. The Cairo City and Canal Company had Eastern money in it; the scheme of a city at the confluence of the Ohio and Mississippi rivers rested on leasing lots. Litigation followed. When the city was flooded in 1858, an investigative committee was established. As one of six, Neal visited the scene.[32] His writing ability was put to use in *The Past, Present and Future of the City of Cairo, in North America*, which was published in the fall of 1858 in Portland. He was also writing a final novel, *True Womanhood*, that was to appear the following year.[33] He also kept in touch with his Portland friends and protégés, now largely located in New York City. As far back as 1840 he had moved in the journalistic scene there during a spell as editor of the *New World*, with another stint as editor of *Brother Jonathan* in 1843.

Now years later, Ann Stephens had established a close contact with the new publishers of popular fiction, Beadle and Adams. Her *Malaeska, or the Indian Wife of the White Hunter* initiated the series in 1860. Through her efforts Neal was added to their string of writers, producing three dime novels for them. *The White-Faced Pacer* in 1863 was followed by *The Moose-Hunter* the next year, and *Little Moccasin* in 1866, the year that Neal lost his oldest friend John Pierpont to death. The last two of his dime novels are set on the Maine frontier but, in spite of the success of republication, lack qualities of lasting literary value. The aging Neal belonged to an earlier age when a talented amateur could startle the literary world of the new republic. He still wrote, but increasingly it was hackwork to order. Thus he drew up the *Account of the Great Conflagration in Portland, July 4th & 5th, 1866*, the disaster in which he lost his library and the papers from which he had intended to write his memoirs.

Working mostly from memory, therefore, he produced a typically eccentric autobiography, *Wandering Recollections of a Somewhat Busy Life*, the title a deliberate satire of Horace Greeley's 1868 *Recollections of a Busy Life*. Neal's old friend Longfellow had been urging him to write up his life. What Neal produced was an old man's summoning up of long-gone days. The bulk of the book harps back to boyhood and early authorship in Baltimore and England, a focus at least partly justified by those years being the time of the author's chief contributions to the developing literary scene. At about the same time he was also gleaning his memory for an *Atlantic Monthly* series of biographical sketches of Jeremy Bentham, William Blackwood, and John Pierpont. All of these are informed and highly readable biographies, that of Pierpont being the best in its personal warmth and insight.

Neal also collected, in 1870, some of his once popular writings for and about children. His acceptance of association psychology fostered his conviction that the associations of childhood shape the man.[34] In fiction he had demonstrated this belief in the presentation of the characters of Will Adams and the dwarf George in the novel *Errata*. He returned to it in tracing his own character, in *Wandering Recollections*, back to childhood experiences. His interest in writing for children sprang from the same sources. His widely reprinted "Children—What Are They?" had been written[35] when his first two children were of preschool age and a third was expected. He now included this early essay, with his fairy tale of "Goody Gracious! and the Forget-Me-Nots," originally published in 1838, and a new essay "Pickings and Stealings" in a volume entitled *Great Mysteries and Little Plagues*. The new essay was a collection of humorous sayings of children which he felt contained a natural poetry of word play. The title of this 1870 collection captured his own and his age's ambivalent feelings of the inspirational as well as the nuisance value of children. One recalls the same ambivalence in Hawthorne's impossible elfin child Pearl in *The Scarlet Letter*.

When Neal had first written his juvenile pieces, children had, as he observed in the preface, been largely overlooked. But now the great days of *Peck's Bad Boy* (1883) and *Tom Sawyer* (1876) were imminent. Neal had pioneered even before such lesser writers of juvenile books as his fellow townsmen the Abbott brothers had initiated their Little Rollo series (beginning in 1836), and Elijah Kellogg, from his pastorate at the Congregational Church, had produced his Elm Island stories for boys (beginning in 1867). Once again John Neal had been content to break ground and leave the harvest to those who followed.

Only one more publication marked his fast waning career of sixty years. He wrote a guidebook that celebrates the city where he had been the taunted schoolboy, the reviled returning critic, and the finally accepted leader of cultural life. *Portland Illustrated,*[36] historical and statistical in its purposes, is yet brightened with the vivid recollections of its most typical author. It appeared in 1874; two years later, John Neal died, not quite eighty-three.

But something of the vigor and genius of John Neal was transmitted in his family. Of his five children, one—Eleanor—died in infancy; one—James—died of fever at twenty-five. The others inherited his physique and longevity: Mary died in 1914 at age eighty-five; Margaret Eleanor lived unmarried until 1927 when she died at the age of ninety-three; the youngest, John Pierpont Neal, lived until 1915 and the age of seventy-two, when the male line ended, his only son having died in childhood. Neal's family—grandfather, father and mother, uncle James, sister and wife, and all five children—are buried near Neal at Western Cemetery in Portland.

Two of his children had distinguished careers. John Pierpont Neal practiced law with his father until the latter's death, when he moved to Chicago, the scene of a brilliant law career. Neal's eldest child, Mary, married Robert H. Sherwood of New York City. She followed her father as a writer for periodicals and in the 1870s and 1880s developed a career as translator from the French. She translated over forty novels, notably those by Alphonse Daudet, Gustave Flaubert, and Emile Zola. These appeared under the pseudonym of John Stirling. Her descendants are still living. Her eldest daughter Eleanor married Robert Hodges of Baltimore; their only child, named for his grandfather John Neal Hodges, became a colonel in the United States Corps of Engineers, stationed finally in St. Louis, Missouri. His three children include a John Neal Hodges, Jr.

Mary's second child Laura Sherwood married Henry Torry Picking who rose to rear admiral in the United States Navy. Their son Sherwood Picking was a captain in the navy who taught naval tactics for a time at Harvard University. He was killed in 1941 in a plane crash in Scotland on his way to assume a new post as assistant naval attaché in London. He was survived by his widow and two children.

Mary's youngest daughter Margaret married Wilson Patterson of Baltimore, a nephew of the Betsey Patterson who married Jerome Bonaparte, younger brother of Napoleon. Their daughter Marjorie Patterson was an author and actress. She played Shakespeare in London at Stratford-on-Avon in the second decade of this century. Her novels include *Fortunata* (1911), *The Dust of the Road* (1913), and *A Woman's Man* (1919).[37]

CHAPTER 8

Romantic Genius as American

AT the age of eighty-one, John Neal could look back over his writing career and, with the modesty that came with his years, say that "I have written and published in the course of my long life, abroad and at home, what would make at least eighty-one good sized volumes—such as they are."[1] Prolific he had been, especially in his early years, but he remains a writer without a masterpiece; for, as his more perceptive contemporaries agreed, even his best work is marred by haste and lack of organization. He had tried to do too much, and flaws in his education and personality contributed to his unevenness. Certainly, he belonged to the generation of those born too early for the major accomplishments of American letters. Those who followed would produce riper crops from the land he mapped and partially cleared.

He had had his time of boasting and self-aggrandizement: he could in later years see with honesty the quality of his own works—"such as they are." Writing to Elizabeth Oakes Smith in 1856 he assessed his work as he sent material for one of her journals:

> I am sorry to say that in my writings, which it is too late for me to think of suppressing or smothering there is many a line, which "dying" or living, "I should wish to blot."
>
> Many times I have been urged to go over them, with care, and so to deal with them that such portions as I should be willing to have come up in judgment against me hereafter, might be kept in remembrance. If I could trust myself—and perhaps I may—I think it would be wise for me to do so, before it is too late. . . .
>
> Meanwhile I have no objection to seeing now and then, and here and there, some parts of the many volumes I have thrown off, reappear in the magazines of the day, with such alterations as may now seem to me proper and becoming. Herewith I send you a tale and a poem, to begin with. May they help to promote the great purpose to which so many off [sic] us, who are swiftly passing away, have pledged ourselves.[2]

The great purpose to which he alludes in his last sentence is, of course, the cause of literary nationalism for which and in which he labored so tellingly both at home and abroad. By his flamboyant personality and by his writings he had done much to establish the material of America, set forth in the language of America, as the content of a native literature. His most lasting contribution was to the configuration of the Yankee, and he is best judged as a Byronic man of genius as Yankee.

John Neal was a force, a dynamism for those who followed: Longfellow, Poe, Hawthorne, Melville, Whitman, Twain. He had carried literary nationalism into the journals of the opposition, to the British Isles themselves; he had demonstrated how to talk on paper in the real language of America; he had created an image of the American writer as one of individuality and originality; and he had helped to develop the mythical Yankee. In historical fiction dealing with material of the colonies, the frontier, and the Revolution, he was for a time the chief rival of Cooper.[3] His accomplishments were wide, far-reaching, stimulating to others. Now, a hundred years late, the time has arrived for a reevaluation of his work; but for this, a collection of his best tales and articles is needed. Until then, the judgment of Lowell stands unchallenged: "In letters, too soon is as bad as too late;/Could he only have waited he might have been great."

But another charge of Lowell's deserves to be laid to rest. The time was 1848, the American Renaissance was fast outdating Neal's accomplishments. Yet the Portland writer deserved and still got a large section of Lowell's *A Fable for Critics* to himself. But in it the Boston poet sneered at the former Massachusetts province of Maine, leveling a charge of provincialism to explain Neal's failures: "There swaggers John Neal, who has wasted in Maine/The sinews and cords of his pugilist brain." Lowell's slur against Neal's home state has stuck. The charge is echoed by Van Wyck Brooks (1940) who cites Neal as an example of the blighting of talent by an inhospitable literary climate; and by Alexander Cowie (1951) who concludes that after 1830, "he had merely contracted his circle . . . finally no larger than Portland, Maine. . . ."

Even Neal's sympathetic biographer Benjamin Lease (1972) speaks of "the physical isolation that set him apart from the literary ferment of Boston and New York." For Lease as for those before him, Neal's final failure to achieve a major work is laid to his hometown of Portland.[4] Such a charge merits reassessment, for the evidence is far from clear that Neal would have written more—or better—had he

returned from England and settled in New York City as editor of
M. M. Noah's projected magazine as he had first planned. The flaws
of his talent were uniquely his own; and the local milieu in which he
worked was far more cosmopolitan in the first half of the nineteenth
century than ever again.

Between 1800 and 1840 a number of circumstances agreed to make
Portland a regional capital. Its tradition running back to its first
settlement in 1632 lent an air of settled satisfaction, while its position
on the edge of the Maine wilderness and its own gradual recovery
from almost total destruction in 1775 gave it a frontier spirit of
adventure and growth. This fusion of established culture with frontier
conditions, of conservative ideals with situations demanding radical
solutions, resulted in the special intellectual climate into which John
Neal was born and to which he returned in the yeasty days when,
statehood just granted in 1820, the city was the state capital.

The climate there was what Charles Eliot Norton in his perceptive
sketch of Longfellow saw as providing the special seed ground for the
New England Renaissance. Challenging later scholars, Norton wrote
"This condition of Society in New England deserves to be set forth in
much greater detail . . . as accounting in large measure for the spirit
and form of the works of the poets and men of letters who gave
distinction to the country in the middle of the century."[5] Portland
shared in the larger New England culture even for the earlier
generation of Neal. The town of about twenty-five hundred inhabitants into which he was born would in fifty years not only set the pace
for the whole of Maine but almost become "a rival, and not a satellite
of either Boston or New York."[6] The economic success of the peroid
gave the money and leisure that could make possible cultural success
if impetus and talent were available—which, or course, they were.

By 1836 aspirations had been fulfilled. A writer in the *Portland
Magazine* for May 1 of that year could summarize the progress of the
city: "Her buildings and her churches were before me, but they were
but the emblems of her progress;—the substance lay in her men—in
the intellectual endowments of her inhabitants—in her *literature* and
religion. . . ." He could conclude that in a town of fourteen thousand
"we have built up a monument more lasting than brick—more stable
than granite; a monument of intellect, erected by such men as Neal,
Mellen, Longfellow, Willis, Furbish, Carter, Brooks, Ingraham and
a host of others. . . ." Unknown as some of his names are today,
others have their place in the development of American letters. Neal
had not buried himself in Maine nor injured unduly his chances for

success by settling in his home town, certainly not through 1836. It is true that the depression of that year caused a scattering of the literary and artistic circle of Portland, leading many of the group to New York. But he was in close touch by correspondence and extended visits to the larger city. There is no evidence that he would have done better elsewhere.

At the time of the diaspora, Neal had recently inherited from his unmarried uncle the quarries that were to be the cornerstone of his personal fortune in building stone, real estate, insurance. His career after 1840 is that of a public–minded citizen, doing some writing but deeply occupied with his business ventures. As the young journalist James Brooks noted,

The death of an uncle, in leaving him a portion of his estate, has taken away that stimulus that formerly urged him to literary publication, and in some degree made him trifle with his reputation. But he is industrious now—none more so—energetic, cheerful, happy in a family growing up around him, and is every day turning enemies into friends.[7]

Brooks suggests the pleasanter life that opened for John Neal with his inheritance. He used quarry stone to build his Federal style double house on State Street in 1836, filling it with furniture of his own design, and stocking its library shelves with a major collection bound to his specifications. Surrounded by a growing family, accepted as a substantial and even famous citizen, he played a new role of public service. He seemed well satisfied to write reviews, reissue earlier writings, and leave to the younger generation the carrying on of his pioneer literary endeavors. Neal's true accomplishments lay in the years between 1817 and 1835 when he assumed and wore the mantle of genius. He took fire from the shrine of Byron when he burst upon the literary stages of America and then of England as a Yankee extraordinary.

In this somewhat theatrical role of Yankee genius, he impressed his contemporaries by his sheer power. For whatever his achievements lacked in finesse and polish, they struck their readers as a force, evidence, they felt, that the author was a man of innate genius. In the years when Neal was presenting himself in Baltimore as Jehu O'Cataract, the word "power" was the one most often applied to him and his products, a word then commonly associated with genius. Himself aware of his role, he played the scene as a romantic man of genius, subspecies natural Yankee. This quality of the man, or rather the fusion of the man and his works, evoked Poe's praise and led Lowell to couple Neal with Poe as prime examples of American genius.

In an 1845 essay in *Graham's Magazine*, Lowell went to some lengths to define "that indescribable something which men have agreed to call *genius*." Drawing on "the very workings of Nature herself," genius has a magnetism that we feel in its presence, a power and enthusiasm that rises to such "impulsive zeal" that "Great wits are allied to madness only inasmuch as they are possessed and carried away by their demon. . . ." The possession has a fecundity of imagination that opposes genius to talent, which never soars but "sticks fast to earth." Neal, for Lowell, exhibits this quality of genius as Yankee, just as Poe exhibits it as Southerner.[8]

Neal himself had presented the same romantic commonplace as Lowell in his critique of Joseph Dennie in 1824: "Mr. Dennie was not a man of genius—there was nothing remarkable in anything that he ever said or did. He was a man of talent—and (what more can we say?)—*classical*."[9] It was the mark of genius in the new romantic mode (as opposed to the calmer talent of classical writers) that Neal admired in Charles Brockden Brown, Byron, or Maturin, and caused his rejection of Dennie or Irving as too tame by far. He himself would be "remarkable," a titan of the Byron mold—not earthborn but of the stars. How far he succeeded can be seen in the general reaction by those who praised and those who blamed; both agreed on this one point. As Brooks put it, "There *is* genius in his soul. It blazes forth in all his productions. . . . It is wayward and erratic, as well as grand and sublime . . . else it would not be genius." And, continues Brooks, it is American: ". . . Neal is an American, heart and soul. . . . His eye is here among our own rivers, our own hills, and our own boundless wilderness. His books are of an American hue." The power of this American genius has impact upon the reader; his writing "forces us to feel and think—it carries us beyond ourselves."[10] This is the John Neal they knew, inspirer of younger writers and model of the Byron figure transplanted to America.

But romanticism had its dangers of excess and too often to these Neal succumbed. The rejection of classical models placed an undue stress on originality that could easily run to eccentricity. As C. M. Bowra puts it, "A . . . danger lies in the exacting demands which the Romantic outlook makes of its votaries. It insists that a man must exploit to the utmost what is characteristically his own, and especially his individual vision and special inspiration . . . tradition means little to it."[11] In projecting originality, Neal like James Hogg in Scotland, failed to avoid the danger suggested by Bowra; a damaging British review of *Brother Jonathan* spoke of him as "the most original writer of his day,"[12] implying fatal eccentricity.

In rejecting rationalism, romanticism also releases unconscious areas of life as Neal did in his novels of self-justification. To achieve this release, the method of composition was often deliberately that of "o'er hasty" composition, approaching automatic writing. At best, such writing could be exciting and fresh; at worst, it became incoherent rant.[13] Further, the romantic mode allowed—even demanded—the passionate revelation of self. Once again, Byron was Neal's model. Byron's biographer, Leslie Marchand, concludes of the English poet that "no writer was ever more patently autobiographical in the creations of his imagination. . . . even when he deliberately set out to write objectively . . . he could not but make the major figures over into personalities like himself with problems that were his own." In fact, Byron could project in his works of imagination aspects of himself that he might otherwise not have been able to live with: "When he wrote, Byron escaped into an alter ego which was only a part of himself and gave expression to aspects of his nature of which his common sense could not quite approve."[14] Marchand's description of Byron in these quotations could well have been written about the John Neal of the novels of the early 1820s.

A saving element, however, in Neal's espousal of the role of genius lay in his personality. He was a true New Englander, essentially moral, painfully honest, and centrally manly. When adapted to the American climate, the romantic theory of genius was made to incorporate the vigor of moral earnestness. Thus, for Emerson, "the value of genius to us is in the veracity of its report." The genius is true to himself and reports honestly, as did Neal even to the detriment of friendship, if need be. A further key to genius for Emerson is the personality behind the writing; he was announcing in the 1840s, "Talent alone cannot make a writer. There must be a man behind the book. . . ." Indeed, he held that "It makes a great difference to the force of any sentence, whether there be a man behind it, or no."[15] Downright honesty, moral force, manly power were elements of the romantic genius as American, and Neal had these elements, even in excess. He had, said one observer, "a proud heart, an indomitable spirit, a *genius* fitted for any thing and every thing he undertook."[16] As a result, his impact upon his contemporaries was great; he had the power of genius and he had it as a natural man,[17] self-educated and self-propelled upon the world. He had not been formed to the patterns of the schools, but had developed according to his natural proclivities. In strengths and weaknesses, in accomplishments and failures, John Neal was America's natural man, the man of genius in the guise of self-made Yankee. Those who knew him loved him for his successes that vindicated the current doctrine, or attacked him for failures that blazoned weaknesses in the doctrine itself. They could not be neutral, for he was, after all, a Yankee to be reckoned with.

Notes and References

Chapter One

1. James Brooks, "Letters from the East—John Neal," *The New-York Mirror*, October 12, 1833, pp. 117–18.
2. The name of Falmouth was changed to Portland early in the nineteenth century; hereafter reference will be made only to Portland.
3. For details of the Neal and Hall genealogies, I am indebted to the research of my father Albert J. Sears, long-time secretary of the Maine Historical Society.
4. William Willis, *The History of Portland* (Portland, 1865), p. 408.
5. For example, the Quakers in the opening chapters of *The Down-Easters,* in *Brother Jonathan* where their attention to trivia and lack of adaptability are criticized (II, 166–168), and in the tale "The Little Fat Quakeress."
6. Brooks, p. 69.
7. Eyewitness biographical information about Neal may be found in D. C. Colesworthy, *School Is Out* (Boston, 1876), pp. 339–45; John M. Todd, *A Sketch of the Life of John M. Todd* (Portland, 1906), pp. 66–67; and *The Autobiography of Elizabeth Oakes Smith*, ed. Mary Alice Wyman (Lewiston, Maine, 1924). See also the Selected Bibliography below.
8. See my "Portland, Maine, as a Cultural Center, 1800–1840" (Ph.d. diss., Harvard University, 1952).
9. See Donald A. Yerxa, "The Burning of Falmouth, 1775; A Case Study in British Imperial Pacification," *Maine Historical Society Quarterly* 14 (Winter, 1975), 119–61, for an account of the destruction as related to larger issues of the war.
10. See Frederick G. Fassett, Jr., *A History of Newspapers in the District of Maine, 1785–1820* (Orono, Maine, 1932), pp. 123–39.
11. Neal, *Wandering Recollections* (Boston, 1869), p. 47; hereafter cited in text as *WR*.
12. *Autobiography,* pp. 64–65.
13. Clearest evidence of Neal's reading is found explicitly in *Wandering Recollections* and implicitly from his criticism and reviews throughout his career. Unfortunately his extensive private library, started at Baltimore and shipped to Portland, was destroyed in the fire of 1866.
14. *Autobiography,* p. 65.
15. As early as 1801 proprietors' libraries for the well-to-do were supplemented by two lending libraries—those of Jenks and Isaac Adams.

129

Both men were printers and Adams also advertized "Cash given for rags and junk" (Portland *Gazette,* February 16, June 22, 1801). For the reading of the city in his boyhood, see Donald A. Sears, "Libraries and Reading Habits in Early Portland (1763–1836)," *Maine Historical Society Newsletter* 12 (Spring, 1973), 151–65.

16. Manuscript notebook of the Union Social Library, in the Maine Historical Society Library, Portland, Maine.

17. For Neal's early years in Baltimore, see *Wandering Recollections,* especially chapters, 1, 5, and 12; Benjamin Lease, *That Wild Fellow John Neal* (Chicago, 1972), pp. 12–37; Dane Yorke, "Yankee Neal," *The American Mercury* 19 (March, 1930), 361–65; John Earle Uhler, "The Delphian Club," *Maryland Historical Magazine* 20 (1925), 305–46; and Delphian Club Records at the Maryland Historical Society.

18. *The Portico* 3 (1817), 184.

19. Sears, "Portland, Maine, as a Cultural Center," p. 194. The Portland Forensic Club was formed in 1828 but opened its debates to the public the following year when James Furbish, language teacher at the Portland Academy, solicited the aid of John Neal through an open letter addressed to him. From that point the club followed the pattern of the Delphian Club in publishing their essays in a journal, *The Experiment.* The hand of Neal is clearly indicated.

20. Irving T. Richards, "The Life and Works of John Neal" (Ph.D. diss., Harvard University, 1932), I, 182–86, rehearses the topics of the Delphian Club, 1816–1819. The actual essays as well as topics are preserved in the club "archives" in the Maryland Historical Society Library, Baltimore.

21. The reviews in the *Baltimore Patriot* (August 9, 1819) and the *New-England Galaxy* (August 3, 1819) are generally favorable, but Edward Channing in the *North American Review,* 8 (1818), 142–56 judged Neal's poetry irresponsibly eloquent rather than accurate. Still smarting from this rather justified criticism, Neal seldom missed an opportunity to square off against the journal; thus in a review of *The Legendary* in the *Yankee* for June 18, 1828, he writes that his essay is "preeminently North-American-reviewish—with this only difference, that though I have flourished my pocket-handkerchief with a good deal of dignity, I have not done it—as if I were keeping time to the Hallelujah chorus. . . ."

22. Griswold, *Poets and Poetry of America* (Philadelphia, 1842), p. 153.

23. Review of *The Village* in *The Portico* 3 (1817), 169.

24. See William Ellery Leonard, *Byron and Byronism in America* (Boston, 1905), pp. 48–50, for Neal as an American Byron. Leonard finds *Otho* less successful (a "Burlesque exaggeration") than "The Sleeper," a poetic tribute to Byron, and "Niagara," each of which evinces some concrete reality and vividness. "The Sleeper," a long poem in free ode form, was, according to Neal, written the day after the funeral of Byron and appeared in *The Yankee,* April 9, 1828. His review of *Manfred* appeared in *The Portico* 4 (July–

December 1817), 260–74 and of *Bertram* in 3 (January–June 1817), 421–29. Published in Boston, *Otho* was dedicated to "The Delphians."

25. *"Criticism: Manfred," The Portico* 4 (1817), 273.

26. "Lady Byron," *The Revolution* 5 (January 20, 1870), 36–37.

27. The revised version had to wait until 1828 when Neal ran it serially in *The Yankee*.

28. Quotations are from the preface to *Otho*, pp. x–xi. See also *Wandering Recollections*, pp. 222–23.

29. *Wandering Recollections*, p. 187.

30. Ibid., p. 5.

31. Ibid., pp. 4–5.

32. Various joint trips with their wives were planned in later years, but it was not until 1833 that Neal and Pierpont met by chance in a hotel in Buffalo and seized the chance to visit the falls together. The night was marked by an extraordinary shower of stars which they missed by being asleep (*WR*, 8–9).

33. *Wandering Recollections*, pp. 190–192. For another response, see p. 257.

34. See by Neal, "Review of *The Village*," *The Portico* 3 (March, 1817), 169–72; "Criticism: Lord Byron," *The Portico* 2 (1816), 304–15, 476–85; 3 (1817), 173–84; "Criticism: *Manfred*," *The Portico* 4 (1817), 260–74; "Childe Harold's Pilgrimage, Canto Fourth," *The Portico* 5 (1818), 420–38; *Randolph*, II, 23–59; "What Is Poetry? and What Is It Good For?" *Sartain's Union Magazine* 4 (1849), 11–15; Review of *Salome*, in *Putnam's* 1 (1868), 718–22.

For studies of Neal's literary theories, see Benjamin Lease, "Yankee Poetics: John Neal's Theory of Poetry and Fiction," *American Literature* 24 (1953), 505–19; and Joseph J. Rubin, "John Neal's Poetics as an Influence on Whitman and Poe," *New England Quarterly* 14 (1941), 359–62.

35. Review of *The Village*, in *The Portico* 3 (1817), 170.

36. *Randolph*, II, 185–86.

37. "What Is Poetry?", *Sartain's Union Magazine* 4 (January–June, 1849), 11.

38. "Yankee Poetics," *American Literature* 24 (1953), 505–19. His analysis is expanded in his *That Wild Fellow John Neal* (Chicago, 1971), chap. 6.

39. "Marginalia," in *The Complete Works of Edgar Allan Poe*, ed. James A. Harrison (New York, 1907), 16, 152 and quoted by Lease, *That Wild Fellow*, p. 161.

40. Joseph J. Rubin, "John Neal's Poetics," *New England Quarterly*, 14 (June, 1941), 359–60.

41. "American Writers," *Blackwood's* 17 (February 1825), 186–207.

42. Trans. John Black (London, 1815).

43. The importance of Schlegel in the development of American critical theory has been amply documented by Hanna-Beate Schilling, "The Role of the Brothers Schlegel in American Criticism as Found in Selected Periodi-

cals, 1812–1833; A Critical Bibliography," *American Literature* 43 (1972), 563–79. For Poe's indebtedness to Schlegel, see Margaret Alterton, *The Origins of Poe's Critical Theory* (Iowa City, 1925); Albert J. Lubbell, "Poe and A. W. Schlegel," *Journal of English and Germanic Philology* 52 (1953), 1–12; and Michael Allen, *Poe and British Magazine Tradition* (New York, 1969). For Neal and Schlegel, see Benjamin Lease, *That Wild Fellow John Neal* (Chicago, 1972), chap. 6 passim.

44. *Randolph*, II, 25.

45. Selected as one of three examples in George Bancroft Griffith, *The Poets of Maine* (Portland, 1888).

46. *Portland Magazine* 2 (October, 1835), 11.

47. See Donald A. Sears, "Folk-Poetry in Longfellow's Boyhood," *New England Quarterly* 45 (March, 1972), 96–105. Neal's "Cape Cottage" appeared in *The New World* 6 (1843), 47.

48. By George A. Bailey, in Portland *Transcript*, April 21, 1849.

49. Neal's line regarding the American symbol, the eagle, as the "Fierce Gray Bird" was long remembered and quoted; see *Wandering Recollections*, p. 222. The poem itself was long popular for public declamation. While he wrote little poetry after the Baltimore period, an occasional poem appeared in the journals; as late as the December, 1849, issue of *Godey's Magazine and Ladies' Book* appeared his poem "The Firemen's War" (p. 420). Throughout the nineteenth century, Neal's poems continued to appear in anthologies: Samuel Kettel, in *Specimens of American Poetry* (1829), devotes twenty-three pages to Neal; *The Ladies' Amaranth* for 1838 contains three selections of Neal; John Keese, in *The Poets of America* (1840), includes "Birth of a Poet"; Rufus W. Griswold, in *The Poets and Poetry of America*, selects heavily from "The Battle of Niagara"; and George B. Griffith, in *The Poets of Maine* (1888), offers three short poems.

Chapter Two

1. Neal's fiction is discussed by Herbert Ross Brown, *The Sentimental Novel in America 1789–1860* (Durham, North Carolina, 1940, reprinted New York, 1959) for attitudes toward women and the religious novel; by Alexander Cowie, *The Rise of the American Novel* (New York, 1948), pp. 165–77; by David Brion Davis, *Homicide in American Fiction, 1789–1860* (Ithaca, N.Y., 1957) for his Titanic heroes; by Ernest E. Leisy, *The American Historical Novel* (Norman, Oklahoma, 1950) in a brief treatment of *Rachel Dyer;* and by Lillie Deming Loshe, *The Early American Novel 1789–1830* (New York, 1907, reprinted 1958), especially pp. 92–94; and most recently by Henri Petter, *The Early American Novel* (Columbus, Ohio, 1971) and Lease, *That Wild Fellow*, chapters 7–10, 12–13.

2. *Wandering Recollections*, p. 173.

3. Neal, *Keep Cool* (Baltimore, 1817), preface; hereafter cited in text as *KC*.

4. Lease, *That Wild Fellow*, p. 25.

5. Neal to Pierpont, April 17, 1816 (Pierpont Morgan Library, New York); quoted by Lease, p. 24.

6. *Keep Cool*, I, 74–76. Neal developed a similar setting in *The Down-Easters*, making it the scene of a comedy of national manners and an expose of sharpers. Melville developed such a setting further in *The Confidence Man* (1857).

7. His name may be intended to satirize *The Echo*, publication of the Connecticut wits.

8. Neal confesses the falseness of the epigraphs: ". . . inasmuch as it had become a settled fashion to head the chapters of a story with quotations, like those of Sir Walter Scott. . . . I sat down and wrote several pages of dislocated and fantastic verses, which I handed to the printer, with general directions to divide the chapters, according to his own good pleasure, and to prefix the mottoes, without any regard to their applicability . . . no wonder people could never quite satisfy themselves that I was not making fun of the reader" (*WR*, 197).

9. Henri Petter, *The Early American Novel* (Columbus, Ohio, 1971), p. 177.

10. Delphian Club records, quoted by Lease, *That Wild Fellow*, p. 74.

11. See, for example, the prefaces of *Julia* and *Dorval* by Sally Wood, a fellow native of Neal's home state of Maine.

12. Neal, *Seventy-Six* (Baltimore, 1823), II, 228; hereafter cited in text as S.

13. The index was published in Baltimore in 1818. Neal recounts the misery of his hack work at length in *Wandering Recollections* (pp. 210–14). He treated himself to a trip back to Portland with the proceeds.

14. Cary and Lea of Philadelphia brought out the American two-volume edition of *Logan, a Family History* (1822). A four-volume edition appeared in London the following year. As *Logan, the Mingo Chief. A Family History* it was republished in London in 1840 and again in 1845.

15. Letter to Neal, December 18, 1822; reprinted in *Wandering Recollections*, pp. 233.

16. Cowie, p. 167.

17. This scene is the first of several psychologically revealing scenes of a man's midnight visit to a girl's room. Here the "rape" is not only completed but half accepted by the victim (but see discussion in the following chapter).

18. Neal, *Logan* (Philadelphia, 1822), I, 238; hereafter cited in text as *L*.

19. Neal, *The Down-Easters* (New York, 1833), II, 160; hereafter cited in text as *D*. The story of "Bill Frazier—The Fur Trader" appears at the end of that novel (II, 112–72).

20. Compare the Portland burial of Captain William Borrows of the *Enterprise* and Captain Samuel Blythe of the *Boxer*. Both young men were killed in the naval engagement between their brigs on September 5, 1813. The American and British were given full and equal military honors and were buried side by side in Eastern Cemetery on September 8. (See William

Willis, *The History of Portland* [Portland, 1865], pp. 759–60.) The occasion also impressed the very young Longfellow who includes the episode in one stanza of "My Lost Youth."

21. *Blackwood's Magazine* 17 (February, 1825); reprinted in *American Writers,* ed. F. L. Pattee (Durham, North Carolina, 1937); pp. 168–69.

22. *American Writers,* p. 169. For his similar opinion, written in old age, see *WR,* 224.

23. As Neal put it, "I had got charged to the muzzle with the doings of our Revolutionary fathers, while writing my portion of 'Allen's History,' and wanted only the hint, or touch, that Cooper gave in passing, to go off like a Leyden jar . . ." (*WR,* 224). Neal's preceding novel *Logan* had dealt with events on the eve of the Revolution; he now treated the central patriotic period itself, proclaiming on the title page "Our Country!—Right or Wrong."

24. *American Writers,* p. 70. For Neal's use of dialect and development of a colloquial style see Harold C. Martin, "The Colloquial Tradition in the Novel: John Neal," *New England Quarterly* 32 (1959), 455–75; Robert J. Menner, "Two Early Comments on American Dialects," *American Speech* 13 (1938), 8–12; Richard Bridgman, *The Colloquial Style in America* (New York, 1966); and Robert A. Bain, Introduction to *Seventy-Six,* facsimile edition (Bainbridge, N.Y., 1971), pp. xx, xxvi–xxviii.

25. Neal's punctuation was a feature, common to his age, of expressing emotion by free use of dashes and the like. On emotive punctuation, traceable to Sterne, see Ian Watt, *The Rise of the Novel* (London, 1960), pp. 196–97.

26. See Lease, *That Wild Fellow,* p. 95.

27. See below, Chapter 3, section III.

28. Bain, Introduction to *Seventy-Six,* p. xxxiii.

Chapter Three

1. See Lease, *That Wild Fellow,* pp. 34, 47, 97.

2. Neal, *Randolph* (Philadelphia, 1823), II, 35; hereafter cited in text as *R.*

3. See Chapter 1, section IV.

4. See for example Benjamin T. Spencer, *The Quest for Nationality* (Syracuse, N.Y., 1957).

5. The phrase is from Thomas Young and others, *The Literature of the South,* rev. ed. (Chicago, 1968), p. 146. The Pinckney affair is recounted in *Wandering Recollections,* pp. 229–36 and in T. O. Mabbott and F. L. Pleadwell, *The Life and Works of Edward Coote Pinckney* (New York, 1926), pp. 25–29.

6. *Randolph,* II, 256; and Richards, I, 407.

7. See Richards, I, 411–24, and Lease, *That Wild Fellow,* pp. 30–36.

8. Richards, I, 424.

9. *Blackwood's* 17 (February, 1825); reprinted in *American Writers* (Durham, North Carolina, 1937), pp. 187–88. The same statement is in-

cluded in the prefatory material Neal wrote for the Duyckincks' *Cyclopaedia of American Literature*.

10. Neal, *Errata* (New York, 1823), I, xi; hereafter cited in text as *E*.

11. D. C. Colesworthy, *School Is Out* (Boston, 1876), pp. 456–57.

12. See *Wandering Recollections*, 326–28, for Neal's account of being met by Patten's brandished cane.

13. Neal, *Brother Jonathan* (Edinburgh, 1825), II, 240–41, hereafter cited in text as *BJ*.

14. *Homicide in American Fiction* (Ithaca, N. Y., 1957), pp. 278–79.

15. In reaching back for events in his own past, Neal developed a theory of memory that anticipates Proust; he writes:

. . . each sense has its memory; each faculty, its retentiveness—its reminiscence; a mode of receiving and communicating impressions peculiar to itself. The mind slumbers.—The memory of abstract thought dies away. But the senses are startled into exquisite life, years and years, after the mind has lost its hold upon things, by some sweet perfume; some cadence; some vapour; some touch; and some taste; some colour, or expression. (*E*, I, 89–90)

The memory of the senses when applied by Neal to the process of writing autobiography helps to account for the vividness with which his own *Wandering Recollections* recalls events of fifty years past.

16. Colesworthy, pp. 343–44.

17. See Lease, *That Wild Fellow*, pp. 28–34.

18. The Neal-Pierpont correspondence is at the Pierpont Morgan Library, New York. Lease, pp. 30–37, reprints key passages to which this discussion is indebted. Both Lease and Richards (I, 406–24) discuss the Abby Lord and other episodes of Neal's bachelor days from the point of view of tracing autobiographical passages in the novels.

Further references to the correspondence are made by date in the text.

19. See Lease, *That Wild Fellow*, p. 29.

20. *Wandering Recollections*, p. 357; Lease, p. 32.

21. Lease, p. 33. The comparison to drinking is interesting, for Charles E. Rosenberg ("Sexuality, Class and Role in 19th-Century America," *American Quarterly* 25 [May, 1973], 131–53), in tracing the increasing sexual repression after 1830, connects teetotalism with sexual continence. Neal's comparison is revelatory of his middle-of-the-road temperance in both areas. See Chapter 6.

22. Rosenberg, p. 139.

23. See Ronald G. Walters, "The Erotic South: Civilization and Sexuality in American Abolition," *American Quarterly* 25 (May, 1973), 177–201, and especially pp. 189–190 for the "perfect self-control" of Theodore Dwight Weld and Angelina Grimke in their courtship and marriage.

24. The novel runs through 5 (1843), 202–5, 361–63, 447–48, 475–77; 6 (1843), 1–4, 29–33, 132–35, 161–62, 172–75, 197–201, 253–58, 281–86, 337–43, 365–68, 393–96; it is hereafter cited in text as *RE*.

25. *The Prose Writers of America*, 3rd ed. rev. (Philadelphia, 1849), p. 315.

26. The words and those in the following paragraph are those of Molton in his sexual confession in *Randolph* (I, 303), but the parallel to the Neal-Howard affair is too exact. Compare *Yankee* (I, 135) and *Wandering Recollections*, pp. 339–40, as well as discussion earlier in this chapter.

27. See *Brother Jonathan* for another trio, that time involving a married woman and two men.

28. See "Yankee Notions," *London Magazine*, n.s. 4 (1826), 446–47, for this disillusionment.

Chapter Four

1. The letter, in the University of Pennsylvania Library, is quoted by Lease, *That Wild Fellow*, p. 43.

2. These paragraphs are indebted to Lease, pp. 38–66, where he contributes new light on Neal's years in England, especially in his relationship to *Blackwood's*. For other details of Neal's experience in England, see Robert E. Spiller, *The American in England During the First Half Century of Independence* (New York, 1926), pp. 310–14; Fred Lewis Pattee, Introduction to *American Writers* (Durham, North Carolina, 1937), pp. 3–26; as well as Neal's *Wandering Recollections*, pp. 239–322, and article "London Forty Years Ago," *Atlantic Monthly* 18 (August, 1866), 224–36.

3. An anonymous article in *Pen and Pencil* (New York), 1 (1867), 13–15, compares Neal's "impromptu and facile pen" to Wilson's.

4. For the style of journalism developed by *Blackwood's* (and carried on by Neal and Poe in America, and Bulwer in London), see Michael Allen, *Poe and the British Magazine Tradition* (New York, 1969), esp. pp. 3–73. An excellent summary view of early nineteenth-century literary periodicals in England and Scotland is presented in the Introduction to *Romantic Perspectives*, ed. Patricia Hodgart and Theodore Redpath (New York, 1964).

5. See Allen, pp. 41, 47–48, 56, 61–62 for discussion of these traits.

6. Introduction to *American Writers* (Durham, North Carolina, 1937), p. 23. Neal's articles from *Blackwood's* are reprinted in Pattee's volume.

7. Spiller, p. 314.

8. Unidentified clipping in Neal's scrapbook, Houghton Library, Harvard University; quoted by Lease, pp. 98–99.

9. *Brother Jonathan: or, The New Englanders* is discussed by Lease, pp. 55–59, and 107–20, where the Blackwood correspondence is rehearsed in detail. See also *Wandering Recollections*, pp. 239, 254–55.

10. See Mitford M. Mathews, ed., *A Dictionary of Americanisms on Historical Principles* (Chicago, 1951), entries for "Brother Jonathan" and "Uncle Sam." The epithet was still current when the steamer *Brother Jonathan* was wrecked off Crescent City, California, on July 30, 1865.

11. See Lease, pp. 38–66; Alexander Cowie, *The Rise of the American*

Novel (New York, 1948), pp. 171–73; Harold Martin, "The Colloquial Tradition in the Novel: John Neal," *New England Quarterly* 32 (1959), 455–75; and Robert J. Menner, "Two Early Comments on American Dialects," *American Speech* 13 (February, 1938), 8–12.

12. Letter dated September 1, 1825, in the National Library of Scotland; quoted by Lease, p. 116.

13. See *Brother Jonathan*, I, 379–380 and discussion by Martin.

14. Letter dated September 28, 1825, in National Library of Scotland; quoted by Lease, p. 119.

15. The phrase is that of Richard Rush, American minister to Great Britain, in his *Residence at the Court of London*. For Neal's experience with Benthamism, see Peter J. King, "John Neal as Benthamite," *New England Quarterly* 39 (1966), 47–65; Benjamin Lease, "John Neal's Quarrel with the Westminster Review," *American Literature* 26 (1954), 86–88; and also Neal, Introduction to *Principles of Legislation: From the MS. of Jeremy Bentham* (Boston, 1830), pp. 2–147, as well as *Wandering Recollections*, pp. 51–57, 273–95, 300–301.

16. According to King, p. 47, Burr and Governor William Plumer of New Hampshire were among the first Americans attracted to Bentham's ideas.

17. King, pp. 47–48; *Wandering Recollections*, p. 301. Publication of Neal's translation had to wait until 1830 and even then covered only part of the original work.

18. *Principles of Legislation*, p. 59.

19. The article appears in *Westminster Review* 5 (January, 1826), 173–201. The interpolated passage is reprinted by King, p. 51, and is rehearsed by Lease, "John Neal's Quarrel."

Chapter Five

1. For all his projection of himself as a hardheaded Yankee, Neal was peculiarly sympathetic to the possibilities even of witchcraft (see *Rachel Dyer*, p. 24). His Quaker upbringing had exposed him to those who related the inner light to psychic phenomena. His mother felt herself to have second sight, recalling a vision of a disembodied hand on the eve of the death of her husband. Neal made frequent use of such phenomena in his novels; for example, mysterious rappings precede the death of the father in *Seventy-Six*, and the other novels abound in examples of the power of friendship in giving psychic warning of impending danger. He was also interested in mesmerism and phrenology, and wrote articles on them; and he was certainly of an open mind about the psychic. See, for example, *The Down-Easters*, II, 42.

2. Neal reprints pertinent historical documents at the end of the novel, drawing on the recently republished Calef's *More Wonders of the Invisible World* (1832). His objective sympathy with both victim and deluded causes Cowie to speak of Neal as a "genuine student of early American history."

3. Preface to *Rachel Dyer*, p. iv; hereafter cited in text as *RD*. Neal is, of

course, referring to the extravaganza and rant of his early novels, but the implication of a broader apology seems likely.

4. Quotations are from the "Unpublished Preface," pp. viii–xi. In his emphasis on originality Neal may be compared to the Scottish writer James Hogg (1770–1835) whose fiction also is marred by his avowed belief in "the fire and rapidity of true genius," boasting that he wrote without plan and never revised. He cultivated his originality, was fascinated by the supernatural, and, like Neal, found himself misunderstood and friendless on return to his home town. Both Hogg and Neal received little formal schooling, worked at odd jobs before storming into literary careers, and both were adopted by *Blackwood's* for a period before being dropped. Hogg was associated with the magazine from 1816 to about 1822, just before Neal arrived to replace him as an original in their stable of writers. The firm also published novels by each man.

5. Quotations are from the Preface to *Rachel Dyer*.

6. See his satire of law jargon in various novels, but especially in the trial scenes of *True Womanhood* and in his "Law and Lawyers," *Graham's Magazine* 40 (March, 1852), 254–66, where he hits at the abuse of dead law language.

7. See especially *Seventy-Six*, I, 247.

8. Ernest E. Leisy, *The American Historical Novel* (Norman, Oklahoma, 1950), p. 46.

9. G. Harrison Orians, "New England Witchcraft in Fiction," *American Literature* 2 (1930–1931), 54–71, discusses the anonymous serial novel which was published in *The New York Literary Journal and Belle-Lettres Repository* for September–October, 1820, plus three novels published in 1823, 1824, and 1825 that had scenes of witches and witch trials; only the first, however, is laid in Salem.

10. Indian witchcraft was used by Neal in *Brother Jonathan* (1825). He also returned to the material of *Rachel Dyer* in "New England Witchcraft," *New Yorker* 16 (1839), 337, 345–46, 353–54, 361–62, 369–70 where he asserts that New England still has witches about which he narrates a "true story." The remainder of the article is an undistinguished recounting of the historical material presented in his novel.

11. *Authorship, A Tale* (Boston, 1830); hereafter cited in text as *A*. It is discussed at length by Lease, *That Wild Fellow*, pp. 147–52.

12. Neal never could resist a pun. He lectured to the Delphian Club on jokes and puns (see Records for April 3, 1819, as discussed by Lease, p. 18); included puns ("Teaser" for "Tsar," for example) in *Seventy-Six* and other novels; and published a "Lecture on Verbicide" (*Monthly Magazine*, n.s. [April, 1826], pp. 363–69) which was amusingly structured as a parody of a law article but on the topic of punning. As late as *Wandering Recollections*, he relished his granddaughter's thinking he was writing "a naughty biography" and refers to an early Baltimore paper as "published weakly." These puns

have not worn well and probably never enhanced Neal's reputation as author.

13. *Whittier on Writers and Writing,* ed. E. H. Cady and H. H. Clark (Syracuse, N. Y., 1950), p. 42.

14. See his postscript to Preface to *The Down-Easters* (N. Y., 1833), I, viii. His first use of a boat as the setting to present a cast of varied characters occurs in *Keep Cool,* I, 74–76.

15. Compare the setting of Poe's "The Fall of the House of Usher" with *The Down-Easters,* II, 44–47.

16. Harold C. Martin, "The Colloquial Tradition in the Novel: John Neal," New England Quarterly 32 (December, 1959), 472.

17. See Lease, *That Wild Fellow,* pp. 152, 158.

18. For a discussion of the development of the Yankee in folklore and fiction, see Daniel Hoffman, *Form and Fable in American Fiction* (New York, 1965), chap. 1, Sec. 3.

19. "Reply to Mr. Mathews, by a Native Yankee," *The European Magazine and London Review,* n.s. 2 (1826), 179–87. He had previously lambasted Mathew's travel book on America for inaccuracy.

20. See *Wandering Recollections,* p. 313.

21. *The Yankee,* June 4, 1828.

22. See *The Yankee,* July 2, 1828.

23. *The Yankee,* August 6, 1828.

24. William Charvat, *The Origins of American Critical Thought 1810–1835* (Philadelphia, 1936), pp. 123–24. Charvat correctly sees these remarks of Neal's as evidence of Scottish philosophy and criticism upon American critical thought.

25. See *Wandering Recollections,* pp. 312–13. Neal contributed a letter about William Pelby to the *New England Galaxy* 5 (June 28, 1822); and about Charles Mathews and his Yankee roles in 7 (May 28, 1824).

26. New York *Mirror,* November 22, 1834.

27. See the playbill in the Harvard Theater Collection; also *Eastern Argus,* July 16 and 18, 1834. Seba Smith, the creator of Jack Downing, was an editor in Portland at this time. His wife Elizabeth Oakes Smith was Neal's protegée.

28. Issues of May 16, May 23, May 30, June 6, June 13, 1835. A letter from G. H. Hill, dated April 20, 1835, returns the manuscript to Neal as "too long—too many Yankee's [*sic*] in it and lacks Dramatick incident—" (printed in Richards, vol. 3).

29. See *W. R.,* pp. 124–25 as well as autobiographical passages in *Errata.*

30. Italics added to highlight dialect words and idioms.

31. James Brooks, "Letters from the East—John Neal," *The New York Mirror,* 11 (August 31, 1833), p. 69.

32. On the whole, Neal had the greater fame in the 1830s: his "Animal Magnetism" had column 1, page 1 over Hawthorne's "The Gray Champion" in column 3 of the *New York Mirror* issue of February 23, 1839. Five of Neal's

stories appeared in *The Token* between 1829 and 1836. Even in the next decade, Poe could write, "In the higher requisites of composition, John Neal's magazine stories excel—I mean in vigor of thought, picturesque combination of incidents and so forth. . . ." Poe downgrades Simms and Irving, and adds to the names of Hawthorne and Neal only those of Charles W. Webber and N. P. Willis as writers of fine tales. (See Poe's review of "Twice-Told Tales," *Graham's Magazine,* May, 1842.)

33. See Lease, *That Wild Fellow,* p. 180–81, for an account of the fight.

34. In the *Jahrbuch für Amerikastudien* 12 (1967).

35. *That Wild Fellow,* p. 159.

36. See his "Story-Telling," *New-England Magazine* 8 (January 1835), 1–4. The same essay goes on to give insight into his use of a steamboat setting for *The Down-Easters* when he claims that the best stories are told on stage coaches and steamboats (p. 5).

37. A full list of Neal's stories is given in the Selected Bibliography.

Chapter Six

1. Neal's interest in women's rights is treated by Windsor Daggett, "John Neal of Portland, the First American Lecturer to Advocate the Rights of Women," in *A Down-East Yankee from the District of Maine* (Portland, 1920), pp. 30–40; Boyd Guest, "John Neal and 'Women's Rights and Women's Wrongs,' " *New England Quarterly* 18 (December, 1945), 508–15; Elizabeth Oakes Smith, *Autobiography,* ed. Mary Alice Wyman (Lewiston, Maine, 1924), pp. 68–70; Augusta Genevieve Violette, *Economic Feminism in American Literature Prior to 1848* (Orono, Maine, 1925), pp. 57–60; and Richard Hallet, "John Neal and Woman Suffrage," Portland *Sunday Telegram,* May 22, 1949. See also Neal's *Wandering Recollections,* esp. pp. 62–64, 410–20, 431.

2. Information in this paragraph is largely drawn from Daggett.

3. Letter from John Neal to Elizabeth Oakes Smith, dated Portland, March 11, 1846, in the Maine Historical Society library.

4. Letter to Neal, January 10, 1838, in the Houghton Library, Harvard; quoted by Lease, *That Wild Fellow,* p. 195. For his addresses where she was teaching, see *Memoirs of Margaret Fuller Ossoli* (Boston, 1852), I, 181–82.

5. Smith, p. 68.

6. For the rivalry of these "newspaper" literary journals, see Frank Luther Mott, *Golden Multitudes* (New York, 1947), pp. 76–79. Neal had previously acted for a short while as editor of the *New World.*

7. Quotations are from Smith, pp. 68–69. Charles F. Hoffman was the first editor of the *Knickerbocker.*

8. Neal's activities in New York on behalf of women's rights are treated in full by Daggett, to which this section is indebted. Neal's text is reprinted in the same work on pp. 41–51. Neal was no newcomer to the New York lecture stage. *The Mirror* for December 7, 1839, lists as New York Lyceum speakers

M. M. Noah, Horace Mann, John Neal, and his friend Rembrandt Peale among others.

9. Quoted by Daggett, p. 37.

10. Neal, *True Womanhood* (Boston, 1859), p. 334, italics added; hereafter cited in text as *T*.

11. See Lease, pp. 198–99, who does little with its merits as social history or as a feminist document; other critics have virtually ignored the novel. In *Wandering Recollections*, pp. 405–06, Neal provides personal background to the social tensions that figure in the novel. He was, for example, a participant in the first night of the Astor House riots in 1858, standing on the edge of his box and shouting support of Macready against the crowd's cheers for the popular American actor Forrest. Also in the novel Uncle George (pp. 147–48) is caught in stock dealing with railroads and the development of Cairo, Illinois; compare Neal's own involvement in Cairo and his defense in *The Past, Present and Future of the City of Cairo . . .* (Portland, 1858).

12. See *The Proceedings of the Woman's Rights Convention, Held at Syracuse, September 8th, 9th & 10th, 1852* (Syracuse, N. Y., 1852), pp. 24–28; and Neal's articles in 1869 issues of *The Revolution* (New York).

13. *Wandering Recollections*, p. 390.

14. 1 (1826), 375, 430–32, 699–701; 2 (1827), 55–56. See also *Wandering Recollections*, pp. 116, 333–36, and Smith, *Autobiography*, p. 68.

15. For Neal on temperance, see *Address Delivered before the Portland Association for the Promotion of Temperance, February 11, 1829* (Portland, 1829), also reprinted in part in *Ladies Miscellany* (Salem), 1 (August 18, 1829), 133–34; "Robert Steele. A New England Story" in *The Down-Easters* (New York, 1833), II, 173–204, and reprinted in *Mrs. Stephens' Illustrated New Monthly* (New York), 2 (January–June 1857); "The Temperance Meeting" (report by Ann Stephens, the editor, of Neal's address defending wine), in *The Portland Magazine* 2 (April, 1836), 222–24; and *Wandering Recollections*, chap. 20. The connection between the gymnastics movement and abolition is suggested by Ronald G. Walters, "The Erotic South," *American Quarterly* 25 (May, 1973), 197.

16. Ann Stephens, herself a teetotaler, reports with pleasure and surprise at the courtesy with which the debate was held and though not awed by Neal's scientific facts and statistics, succumbed to his biblical argument that wine is indeed allowed by Scripture.

17. For a fuller account, see Lease, *That Wild Fellow*, pp. 196–98.

18. In 1764 there were forty-four Negroes in a population of about 3,800 residing in Portland; by the census of 1830, the number of "free colored persons" had risen to 314 out of 12,600. See William Willis, *The History of Portland* (Portland, 1865), pp. 440, n. and 768–69.

19. The passage occurs in *The Down-Easters*, I, 65–70.

20. See Lease, p. 126, n. Garrison had also been among those editors to attack Neal for his *Blackwood's* articles.

21. A full account may be read in *Wandering Recollections,* pp. 329–31, 334–35.

22. Ibid., p. 335.

Chapter Seven

1. See Selected Bibliography for list of periodicals edited by Neal.

2. See Frank Luther Mott, *A History of American Magazines* (Cambridge, Massachusetts, 1957), I, 293–96.

3. *Blackwood's Edinburgh Magazine* 17 (February, 1825), 190.

4. Launched at Portland, *The Yankee* merged on August 20, 1828, into *The Yankee and Boston Literary Gazette.* It remained a weekly through June, 1829, issuing a new series of monthly copies from July through December, 1829, when it expired.

5. Charles Holden, in Joseph Griffin, *History of the Press in Maine* (Brunswick, 1872), p. 56. Holden (1804–1875) was an early printer and later state senator who contributed articles on the press of Portland to Griffin.

6. *Yankee* 1 (February 6, 1828), 48, so printed in error for p. 42.

7. Neal, *Portland Illustrated* (Portland, 1874), p. 54.

8. Boston *Morning Post,* May 16, 1840, quoted by Peter King, "John Neal as a Benthamite," *New England Quarterly* 39 (1966), 65. For Neal's residence with Bentham, see Chapter 4, section III.

9. Dated "10th Mo., 1828" and reprinted in Richards, I, 610–11.

10. Manuscript letter of September 4, 1829, at the Essex Institute, Boston; quoted by John A. Pollard, "John Neal; Doctor of American Literature," *Bulletin of the Friends Historical Association* 32 (1943), 10–11,

11. The letter was sent from Baltimore in late 1829; it appears in *The Letters of Edgar Allan Poe,* ed. John Ward Ostrom (Cambridge, Massachusetts, 1948), I, 32–33.

12. The extracts and praise appear on pp. 295–98.

13. For probable influence of Neal's theory of effect, see Lease, pp. 130–32; Walter Blair, "Poe's Conception of Incident and Tone in the Tale," *Modern Philology* 41 (1944), 228–40; and J. J. Rubin, "John Neal's Poetics as an Influence on Whitman and Poe," *New England Quarterly* 14 (1941), 359–62.

14. Letter to Neal dated Philadelphia, June 4, 1840, in Ostrom, I, 138.

15. "Letters from the East—John Neal," *The New-York Mirror* 2 (1833), 69.

16. See *Wandering Recollections,* 38–39, 108, as well as *Randolph,* II, 82–84.

17. Neal's observations on art and artists, chiefly American, appeared in *Randolph,* in *Blackwood's* during 1824–1825, in *The Atlantic Monthly* during 1868–1869, as well as in *The Yankee* and *Brother Jonathan* (the journal) during his editorships.

The bulk of this material has been collected by Harold Edward Dickson, in his edition of *Observations on American Art: Selections from the Writings of John Neal (1793–1876)* (State College, Pa., 1943).

18. Dickson, p. xxii.

19. Portland *Argus*, March 31, 1825.

20. See Jean Lipman, "Rufus Porter, Yankee Wall Painter," in *Art in America* (Springfield, Mass., 1950), pp. 173–76.

21. See *Portland Magazine*, January 1, 1835, pp. 21–23; *Atlantic Monthly* 22 (December, 1868), 641–50; and Neal, *Portland Illustrated* (Portland, 1874), pp. 28–29.

22. In 1835 Neal speaks of the wall paintings in the past tense. An unidentified clipping dated 1895 in the files of the Maine Historical Society library states that Codman also decorated the walls of the Charles Frost House in Stroudwater.

23. *Portland Magazine*, January, 1835, p. 122.

24. It is apparently this picture that was exhibited at the Boston Athenaeum in 1830 as "#95 Landscape . . . A Composition, owned by Mr. Deblois, Portland."

25. *Portland Illustrated*, p. 30.

26. See *Yankee*, February 6, 1828, p. 48.

27. The only such attempt that I have discovered is the single still life exhibited at the Boston Athenaeum in 1830.

28. Oliver W. Larkin, *Art and Life in America* (New York, 1949), p. 201, makes a one-sentence mention of Codman, referring to his individualized trees.

29. *Portland Magazine*, p. 245.

30. So claimed by Elizabeth McCausland, "A Selected Bibliography on American Painting and Sculpture from Colonial Times to the Present," *Magazine of Art* 39 (1946), 329–49.

31. Quoted by Lease, p. vi.

32. John M. Landsden, *A History of the City of Cairo, Illinois* (Chicago, 1910), chap. 5.

33. See discussion in Chapter 6, section III.

34. See *Wandering Recollections*, p. 38, as well as early chapters.

35. The publishing of this and his other works for and about children span a third of a century.

36. His writings about his hometown also include *City of Portland: Being a General Review of . . . the Subject of a City Government* (Portland, 1829).

37. Information in the above paragraphs on Neal's descendants were kindly researched by my father, Albert J. Sears.

Chapter Eight

1. *Portland Illustrated* (Portland, 1874), p. 54.

2. Manuscript letter, dated at Portland, August 12, 1856, at the Maine Historical Society library.

3. Of the 142 American novels listed by Lillie Loshe in *The Early American Novel, 1789–1830* (New York, 1907), eight are by Neal, ten by Cooper, and eight by Charles Brockden Brown.

4. The strongest charge against Portland was leveled by a native daughter, Elizabeth Oakes Smith, who was in part justifying her own flight to New York: she wrote: "It is to be regretted that he did not come to New York. Our Nazareths are not the best places for us. We are elbowed too much; we have too much envy and malice to contend with" (*Autobiography*, pp. 67–68).

5. *Henry Wadsworth Longfellow* (Boston, 1907), p. 3.

6. Edward C. Kirkland, *Men, Cities and Transportation* (Cambridge, Massachusetts, 1948), I, 204.

7. James Brooks, "Letters from the East—John Neal," New York *Mirror*, October 12, 1833, p. 118.

8. James Russell Lowell, "Edgar A. Poe," reprinted in *The Works of the Late Edgar Allan Poe*, ed. Rufus A. Griswold (New York, 1856), I, vii–xiii.

9. *Blackwood's* (November, 1824), as reprinted by Fred Lewis Pattee, *American Writers* (Durham, North Carolina, 1937), p. 86.

10. The quotations from James Brooks may be found in the New York *Mirror* 9 (September 21, 1833), 93; and (October 12, 1833), 117.

11. *The Romantic Imagination* (New York, 1961), p. 275.

12. Quoted by Brooks, p. 109.

13. See F. L. Lucas, *The Decline and Fall of the Romantic Ideal* (Cambridge, England 1936), pp. 42–45, for the speed of composition by Sand, Scott, Byron.

14. *Byron's Poetry: A Critical Introduction* (Boston, 1965), pp. 13, 44. For development of the Byronic personality, see Michael Allen, *Poe and the British Magazine Tradition* (New York, 1969), chap. 4.

15. The first Emerson quotation is taken from his essay "The Poet," written in 1842, and published in *Essays*, 2d ser. (1844). The second two occur in his "Goethe" in *Representative Men* (1850) but were included in lectures as early as 1844.

16. Brooks, p. 84; italics added.

17. Ibid., p. 70, sees Neal as a natural man.

Selected Bibliography

PRIMARY SOURCES

1. Books

Keep Cool, a Novel. Written in Hot Weather, by Somebody, M.D.C. &c. &c. &c. 2 vols. Baltimore: Joseph Cushing, 1817.

Battle of Niagara, a Poem, without Notes; and Goldau, or the Maniac Harper. By John O'Cataract. Baltimore: N. G. Maxwell, 1818. 2d. enl. 1819. International, 1978.

Otho: A Tragedy, in Five Acts. Boston: West, Richardson and Lord, 1819. Facsimile, Ann Arbor, Michigan: University Microfilms International, 1977.

Logan, a Family History. 2 vols. Philadelphia: H. C. Carey & I. Lea, 1822. London Editions, 1823, 1840, and 1845.

Seventy-Six. 2 vols. Baltimore: Joseph Robinson, 1823. London editions 1823 and 1840. Facsimile of Baltimore ed., with introduction by Robert A. Bain, Bainbridge, N. Y.: York Mail-Print Co., 1971.

Randolph, A Novel. 2 vols. [Philadelphia], 1823.

Errata; or, the Works of Will. Adams. 2 vols. New York: Published for the Proprietors, 1823.

Brother Jonathan: or, the New Englanders. 3 vols. Edinburgh: William Blackwood, 1825.

Rachel Dyer: a North American Story. Portland: Shirley and Hyde, 1828. Facsimile, with introduction by John D. Seelye. Gainesville, Fla.: Scholars' Facsimiles and Reprints, 1964.

Authorship, a Tale. By a New Englander Over-Sea. Boston: Gray and Bowen. 1830. Facsimile, Ann Arbor, Michigan: University Microfilms International, 1978.

The Down-Easters, &c. &c. &c. 2 vols. New York: Harper & Brothers, 1833.

True Womanhood: A Tale. Boston: Ticknor and Fields. 1859.

Wandering Recollections of a Somewhat Busy Life. Boston: Roberts Brothers. 1869.

2. Tales and Sketches

"Live Yankees; or, the Down Easters at Home." *The Yankee* (1828) seriatim; *Pen and Pencil* 1 (1867), 1–5, 21–23, 41–43, 53–55, 73–75, 85–87, 101–3, 118–19.

"Courtship." *The Yankee*, n.s. 1 (1829), 121–28.

"Otter-Bag, the Oneida Chief." *The Token* (1829), 221–84. Reprinted in

Stories of American Life, edited by Mary Russell Mitford, I, 1–68. London, 1830.

"The Utilitarian." *The Token* (1830), 299–318. Reprinted in *The Free Enquirer* (New York), 3 (January 15, 22, 1831), 93–94, 101–2.

"The Adventurer." *The Token* (1831), 189–212.

"The Haunted Man." *The Atlantic Souvenir* (1832), 221–46.

"David Whicher." *The Token* (1832), 349–72.

"Bill Frazier—the Fur Trader." In *The Down-Easters* (1833), II, 112–72.

"Robert Steele." In *The Down-Easters* (1833), II, 173–204. Reprinted in *Mrs. Stephens' Illustrated New Monthly* 2 (January–June, 1857).

"The Squatter." *The New-England Magazine* 8 (1835), 97–104. Reprinted in *The Literary Gazette* (Concord, N. H.), 1 (1835), 162–63.

"Will the Wizard." *The New-England Magazine* 8 (1835), 194–204.

"The Young Phrenologist." *The Token* (1836), 156–69. Reprinted in *The New-England Galaxy,* October 3, 1835, (with some passages restored); in *Atkinson's Casket* (Philadelphia) (1838), 355–58; and in *Emerson's U. S. Magazine* 5 (July–December, 1857), 307–11.

"The Unchangeable Jew." *Portland Sketch Book* (1836), pp. 168–82.

"Animal Magnetism." *New York Mirror* 16 (1839), 256, 265–66, 273, 281–82, 289–90, 297–98.

"The Runaway." *Godey's Lady's Book* (1839), 100–113.

"Sketches by Lamp-Light—No. I. The Newly Married Man"; "No. II. The New-Englanders"; "No. III. The Three Caps." *The Ladies' Companion* 2 (1839), 12–19, 77–81, 129–32.

"The Switch-Tail Pacer. A Tale of Other Days." *Brother Jonathan* (folio), 1. nos. 22, 24, 25 (December 4, 18, 25, 1841).

"The Ins and the Outs, or the Last of the Bamboozled, by a Disappointed Man." *The Family Companion and Ladies' Mirror* 1 (1841–1842), 13–23.

"The Charcoal-Burners. A Tale." *Brother Jonathan* (quarto), 2 (1842), 102–4, 141–43, 188–91, 272–74, 300–303, 354–57, and errata 298.

"Idiosyncrasies." *Brother Jonathan* (journal), 5 (May 6, July 8, 1843).

"The Little Fat Quakeress; or Match-Making at Philadelphia." *The Columbian Lady's and Gentleman's Magazine* 3 (January–June 1845), 8–15.

"Life Assurance." *The Columbian Lady's and Gentleman's Magazine* 5 (1846), 8–12.

3. Periodicals edited by Neal and to which he contributed

The Portico (Baltimore). June, 1818.

Federal Republican and Baltimore Telegraph. February–July, 1819.

The Yankee (Portland). January–August 13, 1828. Continued as *The Yankee and Boston Literary Gazette* (Boston), August 20–October 15, 1828. New series as a monthly July–December, 1829. Merged into *The New England Galaxy.*

The New England Galaxy (Boston). January–December, 1835.

The New World (New York). January–April, 1840.
Brother Jonathan (New York). May–December, 1843.
Portland Transcript. June 10–July 8, 1848.

4. Contributions (in part) to periodicals
    A. *Collections of criticism*
        DAGGETT, WINSOR P. *A Down-East Yankee from the District of Maine.* Portland, Maine: A. J. Huston, 1920. Includes Neal's Broadway Tabernacle Speech on pp. 41–51, as reprinted from *Brother Jonathan,* June 17, 1843.
        DICKSON, HAROLD EDWARD, ed. *Observations on American Art by John Neal.* State College, Pa.: Pennsylvania State College Studies. No. 12, 1943. A full collection of Neal's most important art criticism.
        PATTEE, FRED LEWIS, ed. *American Writers by John Neal.* Durham, N. C.: Duke University Press, 1937. Collects Neal's criticism of American writers from *Blackwood's Edinburgh Magazine,* 1824–25.
    B. *Selections of poetry*
        GRISWOLD, RUFUS. *Poets and Poetry of America.* Philadelphia: Carey and Hart, 1850.
        KETTELL, SAMUEL. *Specimens of American Poetry.* 3 vols. Boston: S. G. Goodrich and Company, 1829.
        UNTERMEYER, LOUIS. *American Poetry from the Beginning to Whitman.* New York: Harcourt, Brace and Company, 1931. Each of the above anthologies includes poems by Neal.
    C. *Uncollected periodical contributions*
        "Dr. Bowring," *The Knickerbocker* 2 (November, 1833), 358–68.
        Our Ephraim, or the New Englanders, A What-d'ye-call-it? New England Galaxy, May 16, 23, 30, June 6, 13, 1835. An unacted Yankee play, good as a source of Maine dialect.
        "Ruth Elder" (Serial novel) in *Brother Jonathan* 5 (January–June, 1843), 202–15, 361–63, 447–48, 475–77; 6 (July–December, 1843), 1–4, 29–33, 132–35, 161–62, 172–75, 197–201, 253–58, 281–86, 337–43, 365–68, 393–96. A Down-East story of seduction.
        "What is Poetry? And What Is It Good For?" *Sartain's Union Magazine* 4 (January, 1849), 11–15. A statement of Neal's romantic aesthetic.
        "Jeremy Bentham," *Atlantic Monthly* 16 (October, 1865), 575–83.
        "William Blackwood," *Atlantic Monthly* 16 (November, 1865), 660–72.
        "John Pierpont," *Atlantic Monthly* 18 (November, 1866), 649–65.
        Review of *Salome: A Dramatic Poem* by J. C. Heywood. *Putnam's*

Magazine 1 (June, 1868), 718–22. Neal's defense of poetry as proof of man's higher nature.

SECONDARY SOURCES

1. Bibliographies
RICHARDS, IRVING T. "John Neal: A Bibliography." *Jahrbuch für Amerika-studien* 7 (1962), 296–319.

2. Biographies
[BROOKS, JAMES]. *The New York Mirror* 11 (1833–1834), 69–70, 76–77, 84–85, 92–93, 100–101, 109, 117–18. Biography by one of Neal's law students.
LEASE, BENJAMIN. *That Wild Fellow John Neal and the Literary Revolution.* Chicago: University of Chicago Press, 1972. Sheds new light on Neal's years in England while stressing his role in literary nationalism.
RICHARDS, IRVING T. "The Life and Works of John Neal." 4 vols. Ph.D. dissertation, Harvard University, 1932. Fullest account but relatively inaccessible.
YORKE, DANE. "Yankee Neal." *The American Mercury* 19 (January–April, 1930), 361–68. Very readable and sympathetic portrayal.

3. Studies
COWIE, ALEXANDER. *The Rise of the American Novel.* New York: American Book Company, 1948. Contains a full critical discussion of the major novels.
GUEST, BOYD. "John Neal and 'Women's Rights and Women's Wrongs.'" *New England Quarterly* 18 (December, 1945), 508–15. Presents Neal's activity in the women's rights movement.
KING, PETER J. "John Neal as Benthamite." *New England Quarterly* 39 (1966), 47–65. Examines Neal's role as a popularizer of Benthamism in America.
LANG, HANS-JOACHIM. "The Authorship of 'David Whicher.'" *Jahrbuch für Amerikastudien* 7 (1962), 288–93. First assignment of this story from *The Token* to Neal.
———. "Critical essays and stories by John Neal." *Jahrbuch für Amerikastudien* 7 (1962), 204–88. Reassessment of Neal's contribution to the genre of the short story, and examples of his work.
LEASE, BENJAMIN. "Yankee Poetics: John Neal's Theory of Poetry and Fiction." *American Literature* 24 (January, 1953), 505–19. First study of Neal's literary theory and practice as it relates to Schlegel.
———. "The Authorship of 'David Whicher': The Case for John Neal." *Jahrbuch für Amerikastudien* 12 (1967), 124–36. Discussion of the publication of Neal's story and his dealings with Goodrich.
MARTIN, HAROLD C. "The Colloquial Tradition in the Novel: John Neal."

New England Quarterly 32 (December, 1959), 455–75. Credits Neal with pioneer development of American colloquial style.

MENNER, ROBERT J. "Two Early Comments on American Dialects." *American Speech* 13 (February, 1938), 8–12. Earliest study of Neal's use of dialect in his fiction.

RICHARDS, IRVING T. "John Neal's Gleaning in Irvingiana." *American Literature* 8 (May, 1936), 170–79. Presentation of Neal's meeting with Irving, and living in Irving's former rooms in London.

RUBIN, JOSEPH J. "John Neal's Poetics as an Influence on Whitman and Poe." *New England Quarterly* 14 (June, 1941), 359–62. Study of those elements of Neal's literary theory that were developed more fully by the later poets.

YOSHE, LILLIE DEMING. *The Early American Novel.* New York: Columbia University Press, 1907. Pioneer study of the novel of Neal and his contemporaries.

4. Background Studies

CHARVAT, WILLIAM. *The Origins of American Critical Thought, 1810–1835.* Philadelphia: University of Pennsylvania Press, 1936. Reprinted New York: 1961. A good account of the influence of the Scottish reviews on American critical theory.

FRAIBERG, LOUIS. "The Westminster Review and American Literature, 1824–1885." *American Literature* 24 (November, 1952), 310–29. Demonstration of the influence of Benthamite reviewing upon American writers and reviewers.

LEONARD, WILLIAM ELLERY, *Byron and Byronism in America*, New York: Columbia University Press, 1907. Classic study of Byron's influence upon Neal and others.

JOHANNSEN, ALBERT. *The House of Beadle and Adams.* 3 vols. Norman, Okla.: University of Oklahoma Press, 1950. Contains the publishing history of Neal's three dime novels.

MOTT, FRANK LUTHER. *A History of American Magazines, 1741–1850.* New York: D. Appleton and Company 1930. Contains history of the magazines which Neal edited and for which he wrote, and with which he feuded.

OAKES-SMITH, ELIZABETH. *Selections from the Autobiography of Elizabeth Oakes Smith.* Edited by Mary Alice Wyman. Lewiston, Maine: Lewiston Journal Company, 1924. Contains personal recollections of Neal, his mother, and contemporaries by one of his protegees.

PETTER, HENRI. *The Early American Novel.* Athens, Ohio: Ohio State University Press, 1971. Contains a study of *Keep Cool* as it relates to the contemporary novels.

SEARS, DONALD A. "Libraries and Reading Habits in Early Portland." *Maine*

Historical Society Newsletter 12 (Spring, 1973), 151–65. Reading taste
    and availability of books in period of Neal's boyhood.
———. "Portland, Maine, as a Cultural Center, 1800–1836." Ph.D. disserta-
    tion, Harvard University, 1952. Study of the milieu of Neal.
UHLER, JOHN EARLE. "The Delphian Club." *Maryland Historical Magazine*
    20 (December, 1925), 305–46. History of Neal's Baltimore club based on
    the record books.

Index

(The works of John Neal are listed under his name)